ELEANOR ROOSEVELT

AND THE ARTHURDALE EXPERIMENT

Eleanor Roosevelt

and the

Arthurdale Experiment

by Nancy Hoffman

LINNET BOOKS
North Haven, Connecticut

Library of Congress Cataloging-in-Publication Data

Hoffman, Nancy, 1955-
    Eleanor Roosevelt and the Arthurdale experiment / by Nancy Hoffman.
      p. cm.
    Includes bibliographical references (p.) and index.
    ISBN 0-208-02504-9 (lib. bdg. : alk. paper)
    1. Arthurdale (W. Va.)—History—Juvenile literature. 2. Roosevelt,
Eleanor, 1884-1962—Juvenile literature. 3. New Deal, 1933-1939—West
Virginia—Juvenile literature. 4. Scott's Run (W. Va.)—History—Juvenile
literature. 5. Poor—West Virginia—History—20th century—Juvenile
literature. 6. Rural development—West Virginia—History—Juvenile
literature. 7. Presidents' spouses—United States—Biography—Juvenile
literature. [1. Arthurdale (W. Va.)—History. 2. Scott's Run (W. Va.)—History.
3. New Deal, 1933-1939. 4. Roosevelt, Eleanor, 1884-1962] I. Title.
Title.

F249.A78 H64 2001
975.4'82—dc21

                                                        2001018622

The paper in this publication meets the minimum requirements of American
National Standard for Information Sciences—Permanence of Paper for
Printed Library Materials, ANSI Z39.48—1984. ∞

Designed by Carol Sawyer of Rose Design

Printed in the United States of America

*This book is dedicated to the memory of my mother,
Marie T. Hoffman, who was also an admirer
of Eleanor Roosevelt, and to the Green Hills
Critique Group. Thank you Tracy B., Thea G.,
Mary L., Cheryl M., Rosalyn R., and Cheryl Z.,
for your support and encouragement.*

C O N T E N T S

*T*his book could not have been written without the help and support of Arthurdale Heritage, Inc. in Arthurdale, West Virginia; the Roosevelt Institute in Hyde Park, New York; and The Scotts Run museum in Osage, West Virginia.

Special thanks must be given to Deanna Hornyak, executive director of Arthurdale Heritage, Inc. and her assistant, Jennifer Bonnette, who provided me with audio tapes of oral histories of present and former Arthurdale residents, tours of the village, and countless other materials. Arthurdale residents Bob and Edna Day, Annabelle Mayor, Joe Roscoe, and Glenna Williams were kind enough to submit to interviews with me.

A grant from the Roosevelt Institute allowed me the opportunity to look through the papers of First Lady Eleanor Roosevelt and other administration officials involved with Arthurdale and to visit the Roosevelt family home and Val-Kill. Photographs from the Library of Congress are from the Prints and Photographs Division, FSA-OWI Collection.

Paulette Shine, director of the Scotts Run museum, took the time to show me what life is like in Scotts Run now and what it was like in the 1930s. And finally, I wish to thank Sidney Lee for lending me his book *"And the Trees Cried"* and for always answering my questions.

From Out of
the Coal Dust

Old buildings are clustered along a two-lane highway and a rocky creek runs parallel to the road. Heavy autumn rain sometimes causes the creek to swell and flood the small downtown. This is Osage, West Virginia; one of many towns in the heart of the Appalachian Mountains that is within a five-mile stretch of mineral-rich land known as Scotts Run. The Run is a coal-mining area and most of the people living here are children and grandchildren of immigrants from places like Poland, Hungary, and Italy or descendants of African Americans who moved here from the Deep South. "I have never seen a place with so much diversity," says Paulette Shine. "So many people from different races and cultures living and working together peacefully."

One rundown storefront houses the Scotts Run Museum. Paulette is the museum's director. Once a coal miner herself, Shine now explains the history of coal miners and their families in northern West Virginia to local schoolchildren and museum visitors. It is a story about surviving in crowded coal camps, working in dangerous conditions, and struggling against poverty.

Less than twenty miles away, on a pleasant, grass-covered plateau is a place called Arthurdale. Its pretty little homes, many with well-kept gardens and generous yards, make a peaceful picture. The people here have lived in this part of the country for generations. Almost all are white. There is a museum here, too. It is located in a sturdy stone building and is twice the size of the one in Scotts Run. This museum tells a different story—one involving a first lady and an experiment in community life.

These two places surprisingly share the same heritage. Many of their residents even share the same childhood experiences. How did they develop so differently?

Their stories began in a time of stagnant poverty and radical change—the Great Depression of the 1930s. At that time, only one-third of the people in the United States had electricity in their homes. They cooked on coal stoves that often were used to heat their homes. They used the material from old feed sacks to make quilts, dresses, and trousers and when those things wore out, they used what was left to make rag rugs for their floors. Many didn't have indoor plumbing. Being poor during the Depression meant going without things that Americans take for granted today.

When most people think of the Great Depression, they think it started with the stock market crash in October 1929. But the crash of '29 was just one result of the economic trouble that had been brewing since the end of World War I in 1918. After the war, there wasn't a need for so many goods and services. For instance,

This coal-mining family was one of the 160 who moved to a better home and a better life in Arthurdale.   Courtesy of the Library of Congress. Elmer Johnson, photographer.

there wasn't a need for steel to build weapons for the war, so there wasn't a need for so many steelworkers. Without a demand for steel there wasn't a need for so much coal to fire the nation's steel mills, so there wasn't a need for so many coal miners.

As more and more miners were laid off and the possibility for jobs elsewhere dried up, conditions in America's coal camps deteriorated. Scotts Run became one of the worst examples of that deterioration. Coal miners became a new class of people—the rural, industrial poor.

Even though the miners and their families didn't live in big cities, they suffered from crowded conditions and pollution just like poor people living in the inner city.

When people are poor and living in desperate times they often resort to desperate measures. There were many communist organizers in Scotts Run. Communism is a form of government in which economic equality (people sharing a country's wealth equally) takes precedence over individual freedom and human rights. Democracy, which is the basis of the government of the United States, is in direct opposition to the ideals of Communism.

Many politicians worried about communist influences in the coalfields. They felt something had to be done before poor people rebelled against their appalling living conditions as well as the country's system of government. President Franklin Delano Roosevelt was one of those politicians. When FDR became president in March of 1932, he vowed to take action to put people back to work and to help those hit hardest by hard times. Roosevelt and the men of his administration developed a number of governmental programs to do just that. Together these programs were known as the "New Deal."

The New Deal did put many Americans back to work by providing them with jobs in government programs like the Civilian Conservation Corps and the Tennessee Valley Authority. The work was hard but worth it. The workers received fair wages while building needed roads, bridges, and dams which generated electricity for people in many parts of the country. While the president worked from the White House in

Washington, D.C., his wife went out into the country to see conditions firsthand. Scotts Run was one of the many places she visited.

Mrs. Roosevelt had long been interested in helping people improve their lives and their living conditions. She used her influence with her husband to make social changes. It was with her encouragement that the Roosevelt Administration put money into resettlement communities for unemployed industrial workers. Arthurdale was the first of those communities.

Without Scotts Run, Arthurdale would not exist. The poverty of the coal camps gave birth to an experiment in community life spearheaded by the country's involved First Lady, Eleanor Roosevelt.

Living in the Shadow
of Scotts Run

"The damndest cesspool of human
misery I have ever seen."

*—a description of Scotts Run by a writer for
Atlantic Monthly magazine.*

*T*he mining towns that lined Scotts
Run Creek in 1929 were much like other coal industry
villages in West Virginia and all over Appalachia—
ramshackle houses perched upon the sides of narrow
mountain ravines called "hollows" or set flat on flood
plains bordering streams. Steep forested ridges often
blocked the sun's rays. Acid mine drainage colored the
creek water orange. Slate and other coal mine refuse
buried the valley floor.

Coal dust made its way easily through screenless windows into the shacks. Glenna Williams remembers from her childhood how hard it was to get rid of the black soot. No matter how much she, her mother, and her sisters scrubbed, the black gunk came back to darken the furniture and walls in their shanty. Like others on the Run, Glenna's house had neither electricity nor indoor plumbing. On cold winter nights, going to the privy out back became an ordeal. By all accounts it was a depressing place to live and work. This five-mile stretch of coal-mining camps became the symbol of the Great Depression in the coalfields. But Scotts Run didn't start out that way.

❧ *Part of the American Dream* ❧

"They used to tell me I was building a dream
With peace and glory ahead...."

So opens that anthem of America's Great Depression, "Brother, Can You Spare a Dime?" As the song suggests, the people of Scotts Run thought they were building a dream. In fact, at one time Scotts Run had a thriving economy offering jobs to a diverse group of people. It was part of the United States's transformation from a land of rural farms into an industrial giant.

Originally small family farms dotted the hills and valleys. Then in the late nineteenth century, industrialists bought up the area's mineral rights. Scotts Run was found to have one of the most valuable deposits of coal in the country and at the onset of World War I it became

During the Great Depression, many people lost their jobs and some lost their homes. Feelings of despair and hopelessness prevailed. Courtesy of the Franklin D. Roosevelt Library Digital Archives.

one of the most intensively mined coal districts. In 1914, 400 thousand tons of coal were produced in Monongalia County; by 1921, production had increased to 4.4 million tons. In only seven years, the amount of coal mined in and around Scotts Run had increased ten times. "What the future has in store for this remarkable coal field remains to be seen. It has made history in the coal industry since the day it was opened," wrote I.C. White, a West Virginia state geologist in the early 1920s.[1]

Coal was needed for the manufacturing of weapons and other essentials for the war effort. White, like others, was impressed with the industry's rapid growth. With such rapid growth came rapid change. Cassville on Scotts Run was "a sleepy little village that has been there for years," according to an August 1923 article in *Black Diamond,* an industry magazine. "Its residents do not yet comprehend what has taken place in their little community to transform it into a great hive of industry, with rows of dwellings, stores, schools, churches, power houses, generating stations, and tipples [coal screening plants] that lie in an almost unbroken line for five miles."

More mines needed more miners. As a result, the area became crowded with the different languages and different customs of newcomers. Sidney Lee, the son of Jewish immigrants from Poland, remembers selling meat from house to house with his father. "The babbling languages meant nothing to me, although it seemed the customers and my father were enjoying [the conversations]," wrote Lee in his memoirs, *"And the Trees Cried."* According to the 1920 census, approximately 60 percent of the population living on Scotts Run was foreign-born.

Most of Scotts Run's immigrants came from eastern European countries like Hungary, Lithuania, Serbia, and Rumania or Mediterranean countries like Greece and Italy. Also recruited to work on Scotts Run were African Americans from the Deep South. The miners left their homes and came to Scotts Run in hopes of making a better life for themselves and their families. They believed the money they made working in the coalfields would help them realize their dreams.

As a small boy, Sidney Lee lugged groceries up Osage Hill to Mrs. Prestopov. For his efforts he was given quarts of *gorkies* and *kapusta* (pickles and sauerkraut in Russian). "Nobody made pickles equal to hers," he remembers.

The Lee family eventually set up a grocery store in Osage. Sidney's mother could speak to the Polish, Russian, and Slavic customers and Mutt Pavone, an Italian immigrant and meatcutter for the store, could speak to the Italian customers. "Between them these two had most of the population covered," wrote Sidney.[2]

Of the remaining population, 20 percent were relocated African Americans and another 20 percent were whites who had lived in the area for generations. Most of those people also took jobs in the mines to make more money. That is why Glenna Williams's father moved his family to Scotts Run in 1925 from a small farm in Barbour County, West Virginia.

❧ The Boom Goes Bust ❧

Scotts Run's rapid development also led to its quick economic downfall. Coal production peaked in 1923, a few years after World War I ended. Almost immediately after its peak, the bottom fell out. There was no longer a demand for coal to fire the factories that had produced weapons for the war.

Even in good times, coal mining was a dangerous job. Miners could suffocate from the buildup of methane, a colorless, odorless gas found in coal. The workers would carry small birds into the mines—usually canaries—and watch them. If a bird dropped dead of asphyxiation, they knew they had less than a minute to get out of the mine alive. Mothers and children lived with the constant fear that the men in their households would die in shaft cave-ins and mine explosions.

After hearing of two mine explosions in Scotts Run in one day alone, Presbyterian missionary and social worker Mary Behner wrote of the courage of the coal miner: "How cheap life is after all. There is such bravery in the coal camps. One never knows when going into a mine whether he will come out alive—and yet the miner goes in smiling and sometimes even singing—and gladly the families risk their men to help another in distress."[3] Miners would put themselves in danger to save other miners who became trapped inside a mine.

To protect their interests many miners joined a union.

"My dad was a quiet man who believed in the church and the brotherhood of man," says Glenna Williams. "And to him that was the union."

Like many men from Scotts Run, Glenna's father, Jack, became a member of the United Mine Workers of America (UMWA), a union which tried to insure fair wages and safe working conditions for miners. The United States government had brokered a deal between the coal companies and the miners who were officially represented by the UMWA. But after World War I those contracts were no longer honored by the industry.

It wasn't long before the UMWA lost members and by 1928 it had little power to protect coal mine workers. The National Miners Union (NMU), commonly regarded as a front for the Communist Party, tried to organize the miners to fight for better wages and working conditions. In 1931, desperate Scotts Run miners, tired of not being able to feed their families, went out on strike. At that time, working miners made only 22½¢ per ton of coal mined. The coal company wanted to cut that down to 16¢ a ton. Eventually both sides settled on 20¢ a ton. Bituminous coal was valued at $1.54 a ton before delivery in 1931. It cost nearly $2 to transport the coal by train—more than the price of the coal itself.

Five thousand miners at Scotts Run suffered ten years of hard times. "We felt the Great Depression long before Wall Street [did]," says Glenna. The miners' families were trapped in the overcrowded and increasingly deteriorating coal camps. Some stuck because they didn't have the money to move out, some because they lacked the skills to find work elsewhere, and others because they barely spoke English or understood local customs. "We didn't move. We couldn't move," wrote Sidney Lee. "We had no place to move to."[4]

With hard economic times came frustration and prejudice against those who were foreign-born and African American. Some felt the new immigrants were taking away jobs from whites who had lived in the area for generations. On the way home from second grade Sidney Lee was called a "dirty Jew." Confused, Sidney looked at his hands to see if they were indeed dirty. They weren't. He couldn't understand why he was maligned. But he did notice he had something in common with the boy who yelled at him: "One of his shoe soles had a hole in it and a piece of cardboard was visible. So did mine."

The growing poverty and prejudice made life more difficult and often dangerous on Scotts Run. In an October 13, 1932 entry in her journal, Mary Behner wrote of one miner at Pursglove #2 coal camp: "He says the men are determined and that he can't stand up in front of them and tell them to keep cool when their children are starving . . .and [he] said that next week at this time if wage cuts go thru, the men will be breaking in store windows and forcing a way for food."

Many unemployed and working miners were now indebted to industry-run company stores. Miners at Osage could get a fair shake at Lee's Market but for most people on Scotts Run, company stores were the only places to shop for life's necessities. A weekly shopping list might include dried beans, cornmeal, and fatback. The prices were always higher at the company stores but they extended credit, which trapped the miners even further.

Glenna Williams's mother would send her or her younger sister June to the A&P grocery store on the outskirts of Morgantown, across the Monongahela River. Prices there were far lower than at the company store. But as the situation in Scotts Run deteriorated, Jack Williams became more worried about his daughters walking to Morgantown, even in daylight. Eventually he didn't allow Glenna or her sister to leave the shanty at night without an escort.

It was early in the spring of 1930 and Glenna Williams was in eighth grade. She had just won the Golden Horseshoe, a statewide contest on West Virginia history. The prize was a trip to West Virginia's capital in Charleston. "It was the first time I had ridden in a car with windows that rolled up—we called them side 'curtains'," Glenna recalls. When she returned from her two-day trip, she hardly recognized her home: "It was like an armed camp in that valley." It was a strike. Glenna saw picket lines wherever there was an entrance to a mine. "The picketers were on one side and the guys enforcing coal company interests on the other." As the tension increased, shots rang out from both sides.

Glenna often feared for her father's life while he was out on strike. She remembers her mother begging her dad not to go. According to Glenna, like many other miners, her father figured it was "better to die from a shotgun blast than to stand by and watch his children slowly starve."

In the summer of 1932, when Glenna was in high school, she and other children huddled around the radio listening to the news of their fathers marching out of the hollow toward the Monongahela River. The group was met by heavily armed police and a local judge. "Judge Baker met them at the far end of the bridge," says

Glenna. "He talked with them and promised to get them 'milk and shoes' for their children." The miners finally agreed to return to their shanties.

❧ The Promise for Change ❧

Franklin Delano Roosevelt took the oath of office for the presidency of the United States on March 4, 1933. The people had elected in FDR a man who promised great changes for the country by confronting the poverty in which so many suffered. When he began to keep that promise, finally some attention was paid to the plight of miners in America's coalfields.

That year, Lorena Hickok, a former newswoman, good friend, and aide to the new first lady Eleanor Roosevelt, was taken to Scotts Run by Morgantown relief workers. She reported back to the White House on the deplorable conditions she found there: "A gutter along a village street [was] filled with stagnant, filthy water used for drinking, cooking, washing, and everything else imaginable by the inhabitants of ramshackle cabins that most Americans would not have considered fit for pigs. Within these shacks, every night children went to sleep hungry, on piles of bug-infested rags spread on the floor."[5]

Mrs. Roosevelt, a longtime advocate of the underprivileged, wanted to do something to relieve the devastation in Scotts Run. She decided to go to northern West Virginia and see the situation firsthand. It wasn't long after that meeting that the seeds for a new community to be called Arthurdale were sown.

CHAPTER 2

A Boy, His Rabbit, and the First Lady

"To us Arthurdale was 'almost heaven' and
Mrs. Roosevelt was 'our angel'."

—*Glenna Williams*

On August 18, 1933, First Lady Eleanor Roosevelt drove her own car into Morgantown. It would be next to impossible for a first lady today to travel unannounced and without a number of Secret Service people surrounding her. But the 1930s were a different time and Mrs. Roosevelt was a different first lady.

In Morgantown, she was met by Clarence Pickett, head of the American Friends Service Committee (a Quaker relief program), Lorena Hickok, and two local social workers. No one else knew she had come to the area.

Coal mining had always been a difficult occupation, but the added stress of layoffs and strikes made families struggle just to get the bare necessities to live. When Eleanor Roosevelt first visited Scotts Run, many people had no idea who she was, still, they welcomed her into their homes. Courtesy of the Franklin D. Roosevelt Library Digital Archives.

Mrs. Roosevelt visited at least twelve families in Scotts Run, going into hovels where children and their parents were starving. Many wondered who this tall woman wearing a dark blue skirt, crisp white blouse, and white ribbon around her hair was and why she had come. Some were afraid of "the outsider," but most let her into their homes.

The First Lady showed interest in their struggles. They told her of their hopes and fears. Often she took the small babies of the household upon her lap while listening intently to what their mothers had to say.

At one shanty Mrs. Roosevelt found six malnourished children. "They acted as though they were afraid of strangers. I noticed a bowl on the table filled with scraps, the kind that you or I might give to a dog," she recalled. She especially remembered the brother and sister who "gathered enough courage to stand by the door." The little boy was clutching a white rabbit.

> It was evident it was a most cherished pet. The little girl was thin and scrawny, and had a gleam in her eyes as she looked at her brother. Turning to me she said: "He thinks we are not going to eat it, but we are," and at that the small boy fled down the road clutching the rabbit closer than ever.[6]

Upon her return to Washington, the First Lady told that story many times. It became one of her best fundraising tools. After hearing it, FDR's friend William C. Bullitt gave Mrs. Roosevelt a check for $100 in hope that the rabbit could be saved and the family given enough food to survive. It was and they were.

Eleanor Roosevelt continued to hound her wealthy friends and even White House guests for money to help the Scotts Run miners. She took many of them on tours of the area.

> I came to know very well a stream near Morgantown called Scott's Run or Bloody Run because of the violent strikes....in the mines there....I took many, many people to see this village of Jere, West Virginia, along Scott's Run, for it was a good example of what absentee ownership could do as far as human beings were concerned....Some of the children were sub-normal, and I often wondered how any of them grew up....

> It was quite usual to find all the older chil-
> dren sleeping on bags or rags on the floor and the
> mother and father and youngest children in the
> only bed, which might or might not have a mat-
> tress.[7]

Many others worked long and hard without the influence or considerable wealth of the First Lady. Religious missionaries and social workers provided meals, classes for mothers and children, and more. The best known of these was Mary Behner who started "The Shack," a place for miners and their families to go to get all kinds of help. Because of Behner's efforts, Glenna Williams was able to continue her education. Through "The Shack," a benefactor gave the Williams family the 10 to 15¢ a day for Glenna's bus ride to high school in Morgantown.

❧ *Fear of Revolution* ❧

For the First Lady, helping the people on Scotts Run was more than just a need to do good. The Roosevelts, like many other politicians of the time, feared what would happen if something wasn't done to relieve the situation in Scotts Run. Eleanor Roosevelt wrote in a September 1933 column for *Women's Democratic News,*

> It is misery that drives people to the point where
> they are willing to overthrow anything simply
> because life as it is is not worth living any longer. I
> do not believe if most of us knew the conditions

under which some of our brothers and sisters were
living that we would rest complacently until we had
registered the fact that in this country the day is
past when we will continue to live under any governmental system which will produce conditions
such as exist in certain industries and in certain
parts of the country.

The President and First Lady feared sparks of revolution would explode in America's coalfields—specifical-
ly a communist revolution against the United States
government.

Glenna Williams knew there were communist influences in the area. After all, her father belonged to the
National Miners Union—a front for the Communist
Party. "I remember the first time I heard the word
utopia," Glenna says. "It was used in a description of
workers in Communist Russia."

Sidney Lee remembers Communist Party members
posing as West Virginia University students with peti-
tions in an attempt to sign up new party members.

Others were less worried about "the Communist
threat." Two Quaker social workers, Alice Davis and
Nadia Danilevsky, once told Eleanor Roosevelt's friend
Lorena Hickok, the "poor communists" had as much
trouble organizing the beaten-down miners as they did.
According to the women, after years of intense poverty
and struggle, most miners and their families were "just
too tired to respond to revolutionary propaganda or anything else."[8]

Whatever imaginary or real threats existed in
Scotts Run, it was time to do more for the miners and

their families than just give them handouts. They needed a chance to change their lives.

❧ Dealt a New Deal ❧

By the time Franklin Roosevelt became president in 1933, the country was ready for change. People had lived with economic depression for too long. A "buy it now, pay for it later" attitude during the 1920s contributed to the stock market crash of 1929, a time most people think of as the beginning of the Great Depression. But many industrial laborers had felt the economic pain since World War I ended in 1918.

In his inauguration speech, FDR promised "action and action now," in the form of a New Deal for the nation. The new president asked for "broad executive powers to wage a war against the emergency, as great as the powers that would be given to me if we were in fact invaded by a foreign foe" and he was given them.

Roosevelt's New Deal set up a series of government-funded programs designed to battle the problem of poverty and build up the country. The programs would put many people back to work on government projects which helped improve living conditions for many Americans. The Tennessee Valley Authority was one of those projects. Through the TVA, twenty-six dams were built on the Tennessee River and its tributaries. To this day, the harnessed water still provides electricity to much of Tennessee, Alabama, and Kentucky.

The United States had never seen anything like the New Deal before but what it promised was exciting. It was in this atmosphere of welcoming change that the idea for Arthurdale became a reality. As head of the American Friends Service Committee, Clarence Pickett had long suggested moving unemployed miners out of Scotts Run and into an area where they could grow their own food. Mrs. Roosevelt took his suggestion to the president, who loved the idea. In fact, FDR had long thought about developing "homesteading" communities throughout the country. "It's a plan he has talked about ever since I can remember," said the First Lady.[9]

The Arthurdale program was to work like this: the government would buy land, machinery, and livestock for small farms; build homesteader houses and roads; and bring in water and utilities. The people moving into the community—the homesteaders—would have thirty years to pay back the government. It was a lot like having a mortgage or loan to buy a home, only instead of paying back the bank, the homesteaders paid back the government.

This first homesteading community would have 165 families in it. It was only a small percentage of the nearly 3,000 families living in Scotts Run but it was a start. FDR believed eventually millions of families could be resettled into these proposed communities.

On April 17, 1933, President Roosevelt wrote in a letter to Senator George Norris, a Nebraskan Republican who nevertheless supported many of the Democratic president's programs: "I really would like to get one more bill which would allow us to spend $25 million this year to put 25,000 families on farms at an average cost of $1,000 per family. It can be done. Also we would get most of the money back in due time. Will

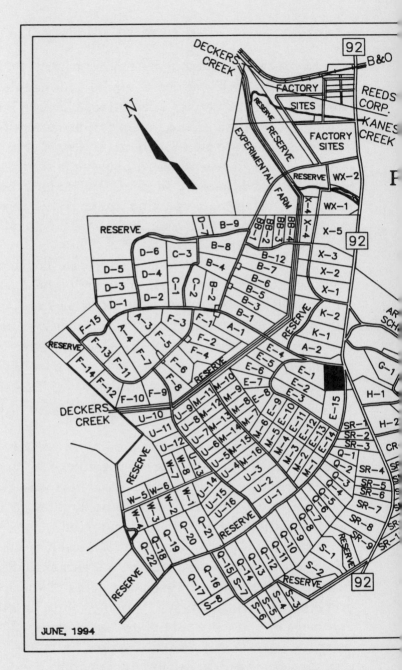

Arthurdale began as a carefully planned community that would be focused around its schools and community center (dark

ARTHURDALE

STON COUNTY, WEST VIRGINIA

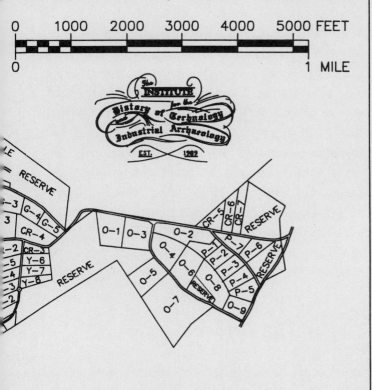

0   1000   2000   3000   4000   5000 FEET

0   1 MILE

COMPUTER GENERATED FROM 1930'S MAP
BY: JOHN T. HRIBLAN II OF I.H.T.I.A.–W.V.U.

square in center of map). Strategically placed reserves insured
room to grow. Courtesy of Arthurdale Heritage, Inc.

you talk it over with some of our fellow dreamers on the Hill?"

Congress agreed and a fund of $25 million was set up to develop "subsistence homesteads" as part of the National Recovery Act. West Virginia was chosen as the first site for such a community.

Eleanor Roosevelt and presidential adviser Louis Howe moved quickly and bought a historic farm owned by Richard Arthur. It had once been owned by George Washington's good friend, John Fairfax of Virginia. Unlike the rough and rocky terrain surrounding nearby Morgantown, the Arthur farm was situated on gently sloping fields of grass. Arthur could no longer pay the taxes on his 1,028-acre farm. So he sold it and its twenty-two-room mansion to the government for $45,000. It would be worth at least ten times that amount today. On June 8, 1934, Mrs. Roosevelt announced to the nation that a new community made up of former Scotts Run miners and their families would be built on the rolling hills of Preston County. It would be known as Arthurdale.

❧ The Chosen ❧

Almost immediately a committee of Quaker and West Virginia University social workers was formed to choose the first fifty families of the new settlement. The committee set up an elaborate screening process. Though named as chairperson, the First Lady had little control over committee procedures. In fact, she disagreed with some of them—including how families were chosen for

Arthurdale. Mrs. Roosevelt had seen the community as "an experiment in ordinary life and an ordinary community contains people of every type of ability and character."[10]

Every applicant answered an eight-page questionnaire designed to determine "moral character, intelligence, perseverance, and foresight." Interviewers checked applicants' neatness, posture, church affiliation, debts, and attitudes.

After applying, Jack Williams, Glenna's father, came home laughing about the ridiculous questions he was asked. The interviewers had showed him pictures of chickens. "Which one is a rooster? Which one is a hen?" Jack howled and thought: It may have been a long time since anybody at Scotts Run had seen a chicken in a pot, but did the folks back in Washington really think they couldn't tell a rooster from a hen?

Other questions included: How do you like best to spend your idle hours? Do you observe any rules in planting determined by the phases of the moon? and What games do you like to play with others?

Other children of Arthurdale's first residents, like Joe Roscoe, don't remember exactly how their families were chosen for this social experiment. But they have vague recollections that the people chosen had to have farming or construction skills.

It became apparent to many early on that the answers to questionnaires and interviews had less to do with who was approved than the race, ethnic background, and political affiliations of those that applied. Almost all the first families of Arthurdale were white and had lived in West Virginia for generations.

Jack Williams couldn't understand why Arthurdale became a haven for whites only. As far as he was concerned, miners from southern and central Europe knew just as much about roosters and hens as he did. What he didn't know was that the politics of the day had entered into the selection process. Southern segregationists had insisted blacks and foreigners be kept out of Arthurdale. There had also been protest meetings in nearby Reedsville about including these people. And apparently to "keep the peace," government officials went along with rigging the selection process.

Mrs. Roosevelt was appalled at the results. After all, she had encouraged 200 African American families to add their names to the list of 600 applicants. Finally accepting her loss on the issue, she requested that the next round of homesteaders be more diverse. She asked the newly formed Homesteader Club of Arthurdale to vote on it. They did, but the results were the same. The group sent a letter to Mrs. Roosevelt giving three reasons for its decision to keep out African Americans and foreigners:

1. The community in which we are located is thoroughly opposed to Negroes as residents, and we feel that we should not risk the loss of the respect we have gained in the community by admitting Negroes.

2. The admission of Negroes would necessitate the establishment of separate schools and churches, as our state laws forbid both races to attend the same schools.

3. Without prejudice to the race, and with the feeling that all races should have equal opportunity, we believe that

those who are clamoring for admission are not Negroes,
but are of mixed blood and far inferior to the real Negroes
who refuse to mix with the white race.[11]

Perhaps the real reason—besides prejudice—that
the first homesteaders rejected African Americans and
foreign-born residents was the animosity leftover from
the days of strikes in Scotts Run. At that time, coal companies recruited many black and foreign miners to work
for lower wages than the striking miners were paid.
Such a tactic is known as "union-busting" and workers
brought in to keep production going were often referred
to as "strike breakers" or "scabs."

In any case, the First Lady lost in her effort to
encourage diversity in Arthurdale. After that initial experience, Mrs. Roosevelt spoke out against racial and ethnic inequality whenever and wherever she ran across it.
But her task at hand was to make Arthurdale a success.

Jack Williams didn't make the first cut of
Arthurdale applicants and his wife worried he wouldn't
make it into the second or third group of homesteaders.
Being a union man all his life and a former member of
the National Miners Union, he might be considered to
have the wrong "attitude." But Jack was known as an
honest and hardworking man. Just as the Williams family had pretty much decided they weren't going to be chosen for Arthurdale, word came that their application had
been approved.

Glenna Williams had little time to think about her
good fortune; there was just too much work to do to get
ready for a new home. She helped her mother clean and
sterilize every piece of furniture they owned. Like other

shanties in their hollow, their house was infested with bed bugs. "We scrubbed everything," Glenna recalls, "and decided to leave all the mattresses behind. We had this couch that turned into a bed and mother tore it completely apart. She disinfected the stuffing and made a new cover for it. Mother was determined this would truly be a new beginning."

Glenna remembers her father loading up their furniture on a crisp October morning. Glenna and her sister June were driven up to the top of a hill in Arthurdale. "It was like dying and going to heaven, like daylight after the dark," remembers Glenna. "Here was this little white house with a backdrop of green trees and there was a lawn and it was brand new and ours." When they went inside there was a kitchen, three bedrooms, a huge living room and most amazing of all—a bathroom complete with a toilet and running water.

"It's hard to say what it meant to us," says Glenna. "But we knew our lives had changed almost overnight."

CHAPTER 3

The Making of
Arthurdale's "Angel"

"We went to her for everything. There was so much
bureaucracy and Mrs. Roosevelt was a constant;
she was our troubleshooter. We all felt we knew her."

—*Glenna Williams*

The first residents of Arthurdale
depended upon First Lady Eleanor Roosevelt and she
came through for them. They remember her as a woman
who accepted them. "We felt Mrs. Roosevelt was truly
interested in people," says Annabelle Mayor, who grew
up in Arthurdale. "She never made you feel uncomfort-
able."

They admired her boundless energy. "She was a go-
getter," says Arthurdale resident Bob Day. "I thought
she was a great lady."

And they were amazed by her courage in taking on the conventions of her day. "She drove her own car," says Glenna. "And the Secret Service men had a hard time keeping track of her."

But the resolute first lady the people of Arthurdale came to know and love had developed through years of personal loss, countless emotional struggles, and the determination to change life for herself and others.

❧ *Grim Beginnings* ❧

Anna Eleanor Roosevelt grew up living in the homes of relatives and boarding schools. She was born in 1884 into a prominent and wealthy family of businessmen, bankers, and politicians. Her godfather and uncle, Theodore Roosevelt, was the youngest man to become president of the United States. Still, Eleanor was a solemn and lonely child. Her mother nicknamed the little girl "Granny," saying she was "such a funny child, so old-fashioned."[12] Young Eleanor hated the nickname. She thought of herself as plain and unattractive and remembered feeling self-conscious about her looks. She said in later years, it was something she "learned to get over."

When she was only eight years old her mother, a great beauty, died of diphtheria; soon afterwards a younger brother succumbed to the same disease. Diphtheria is a bacterial disease and was common and dangerous in the late 1880s before the development and use of vaccinations and antibiotics.

The one person whose company made young Eleanor feel loved and "perfectly happy" was her father,

This picture of an eight-year-old Eleanor between her father and brothers was taken in 1892, just months after she lost her mother. Three-year-old Elliott Jr., right, would soon die also. Gracie Hall, left, would be Eleanor's only sibling to survive to adulthood.   Courtesy of the Franklin D. Roosevelt Library Digital Archives.

Elliott Roosevelt. He was a sensitive, charming, and very troubled man who suffered from serious bouts of alcoholism and depression. Elliott Roosevelt frequently traveled without his family; later he separated from Eleanor's mother.

"Little Nell" is what he called his daughter. Eleanor often dreamed they would live together with her little brother, Hall. But father and daughter had long been kept apart by her parents' unhappy marriage and his misunderstood illness. The lifeline of their relationship had been their letters to each other.

On August 13, 1894, ten-year-old Eleanor Roosevelt received her last letter from Elliott: "What must you think of your Father who has not written in so long... I have after all been very busy, quite ill, at intervals not able to move from my bed for days...Give my love to Grandma and Brudie and all...I hope my little girl is well...Kiss Baby Brudie for me and never forget I love you...." Elliott Roosevelt died during the night of August 14, 1894.

Dreams of a childhood spent with her beloved father also died for Eleanor that night. Her one unfulfilled wish had been "to see father once more," and it remained unfulfilled.

Eleanor and her brother had gone to live with her maternal grandmother, Mary Hall, after their mother's death in 1892. Mrs. Hall had a country mansion overlooking the Hudson River that her family stayed in during the summers. But most of the time, Eleanor's grandmother and four of her grown children lived in a Manhattan townhouse on West 37th Street in New York City. Eleanor's aunts, Pussie and Maude, were beautiful like her mother but spoiled. Her uncles, Vallie and Eddie, were wild and rowdy; frequently they got drunk and shot rifles out the upstairs windows at passersby.

While Mrs. Hall loved Eleanor, she was bound and determined not to spoil her granddaughter as she had her own children. Life in the Hall home was gloomy at best. "There was no place to play games. We ate our suppers in silence. The general attitude was 'don't do this,'" said Eleanor's cousin Corinne Robinson. Corinne described Eleanor's governess as "a terrifying character" and her childhood as "the grimmest ...I had ever known. Who did she have? Nobody."[13]

But despite her bleak upbringing, Eleanor developed a nurturing personality. Like her father she was extremely sensitive to the feelings of others. Beginning when she went away to school, Eleanor wrote her younger brother Hall every day they were separated until the end of his life in 1941.

Eleanor Roosevelt also possessed the discipline her father lacked. She worked hard at her school lessons. Math was difficult for her but she made up her mind to master it and she did. Eleanor loved poetry and writing stories, and while she possessed little musical talent, she practiced her piano regularly.

Eleanor was a shy child. Tall and thin, she had teeth that stuck out of her mouth when she smiled and a small chin. Dressed in the childish and old-fashioned clothes her grandmother picked for her, Eleanor felt particularly awkward at dance school. Wealthy young girls and boys were taught to dance correctly with each other at the classes. Eleanor was sure the other girls were giggling at her clumsiness but she endured the lessons because that was what her grandmother expected her to do.

❦ *Happier Days* ❦

In 1899, when Eleanor was fifteen, her grandmother sent her to school in England at Allenswood, a girls' finishing school just outside of London. Eleanor often called her days there "the happiest of my life."

Courage was something that Eleanor knew her father had admired and it was at Allenswood that courage helped her overcome her shyness. Her growing curiosity about life and the world was inspired by Mademoiselle Marie Souvestre, the school's founder and headmistress. Eleanor once wrote, "Mlle Souvestre shocked me into thinking and that on the whole was very beneficial."[14]

At Allenswood she participated in lively discussions on politics and public affairs. It was during this time that the seeds of Eleanor Roosevelt's social conscience were planted. Mlle. Souvestre became one of the most influential people in her life. The girl was inspired by the headmistress's passion for social reform. According to Eleanor, Mlle. Souvestre "fought seemingly lost causes," but Eleanor also remembered that those causes "were often won in the long run." By the time she was ready to leave the school, the educator wrote Mary Hall that Eleanor "has had the most admirable influence on the school and gained the affection of many, the respect of all. To me personally I feel I lose a dear friend indeed."[15]

Once back at her grandmother's home in New York, Eleanor was encouraged to become a debutante and enter society as many wealthy and prominent young ladies did at the turn of the century. It meant going to endless parties and balls with other young people of the same social and economic class.

Allenswood had changed Eleanor inside and out. Her aunt Corinne said eighteen-year-old Eleanor "looks very smartly in all her pretty French clothes." One of her cousins said she had "never seen anyone so improved in looks" as Eleanor. Despite her improved appearance, Eleanor was bored by the parties; she hated small talk and stiff social situations.[16]

She did find some meaning in the volunteer work she did for the Junior League. The Junior League raised money to build settlement houses to help poor immigrants living in New York City slums. A few debutantes, Eleanor included, wanted to do more than just throw fund-raising parties. They volunteered to work with the people living on Manhattan's Lower East Side. Eleanor taught calisthenics and dancing classes to the daughters of Jewish and Italian immigrants at the Rivington Street Settlement House. At first Eleanor was scared going into the slums: "The dirty streets crowded with foreign-looking people, filled me with terror, but the children interested me enormously. I still remember the glow of pride that ran through me when one of the little girls said her father wanted me to come home with her, as he wanted to give me something because she enjoyed her classes so much."[17]

It was during this time of parties and volunteer work that she was reintroduced to her fifth cousin, Franklin Delano Roosevelt, and at the age of nineteen, her life changed once more.

❦ *Franklin's Wife* ❧

"I am so happy. Oh! so happy & I love you so dearly," Eleanor wrote to Franklin in July of 1904 upon accepting his proposal of marriage. The couple kept their engagement a secret for several months to appease Franklin's mother. Sara Delano Roosevelt felt her son and Eleanor were too young to get married and it took her some time to get used to the idea.

Sara Delano Roosevelt was a domineering mother-in-law to Eleanor. Sara made many decisions concerning the couple's home and family life. Here she is pictured with FDR and Eleanor in Newburgh, New York in 1905. Courtesy of the Franklin D. Roosevelt Library Digital Archives.

Eleanor and Franklin had much in common; they were of the same social class—even the same extended family. They had known each other all their lives; in fact their parents had been good friends. Both had endured lonely childhoods and they shared interests in politics and social reform. Franklin was particularly inspired by Eleanor's uncle, President Teddy Roosevelt. Franklin was tall, thin, and good-looking. Educated at Harvard, he was known to be fun-loving and quite charming. It

was Franklin who initiated the romance between himself and his cousin. He admired Eleanor's mind and her
sincere interest in social causes. From all outside ap-
pearances the match seemed to be a good one.

Franklin and Eleanor married on St. Patrick's Day,
March 17, 1905. Settling into a conventional life for the
time, Eleanor gave birth to six children over ten years—
one of whom died in infancy. Her oldest child, Anna, was
born in 1906. Franklin Jr. died seven months and nine
days after he was born in 1909. A year later in 1910,
Elliott was born. In 1914, Eleanor gave birth to another
baby boy who was also named Franklin Jr. and in 1916
her youngest son, John, was born. During this time,
Franklin became a lawyer and then entered politics.

While all seemed to be going well, Eleanor faced
some of the most difficult trials of her life during this
period.

Franklin's mother, Sara Delano Roosevelt, was an
overbearing woman who was successful in most of her
efforts to run the couple's life. Sara picked their homes,
and had them furnished to her specifications. Eleanor
and Franklin did not share a bedroom. Eleanor's room
at Springwood, Sara's Hyde Park home, was sparsely
decorated and looked like a servant's room. In contrast,
Franklin's bedroom had the best view of the Hudson
River and memorabilia from his life throughout.

Sara Roosevelt's influence on the couple went far
beyond homemaking. She repeatedly told her grandchildren: "I was your real mother, Eleanor merely bore
you."[18]   Eleanor kept her opinions to herself and
repressed her interests in social causes just to get along
with Sara.

The Roosevelt family. From left to right in the top row are Anna, James, and John. Elliott is on FDR's lap and Franklin Jr. sits on the lap of his grandmother, Sara. This picture was taken in June 1919 when FDR was assistant secretary of the Navy. Courtesy of the Franklin D. Roosevelt Library Digital Archives.

Eleanor also had to deal with the deaths of many close family members including her uncle, Teddy Roosevelt, and her grandmother, Mary Hall, at this time. Then in the fall of 1918 something happened which devastated her. Eleanor became aware that Franklin had been having a love affair with her social secretary, Lucy Mercer.

Eleanor was desolate. Her old feelings of inadequacy resurfaced. Her "beautiful" mother had once told Eleanor, "You have no looks, so see to it that you have manners."[19] Now with Franklin's betrayal, she was acutely aware of her plainness, and felt awkward and unloved. She considered asking him for a divorce but after a long time of intense grieving, Eleanor decided to stay in her marriage. She also decided to become independent of her mother-in-law and to once again pursue the causes that interested her. But things between Eleanor and Franklin would never be the same.

❧ *Politician's Partner* ❧

In 1920, Eleanor helped Franklin campaign in an unsuccessful bid for the vice-presidency. It was during this campaign that she gained an unlikely ally in his political adviser, Louis Howe. For years, one of the few things Eleanor and her mother-in-law had agreed on was how revolting Howe looked. He was a chain smoker who seemed to wear the same rumpled suit day in and day out. But on further examination Eleanor found him to be a warm, perceptive, and caring individual who was as passionate about social reform as she was.

It was through Louis Howe that Eleanor Roosevelt realized what an asset she was to a political campaign. Howe recognized her natural empathy and her easy way with people. Eventually he insisted she learn to give speeches. "At first it was the most painful thing I had to do. Now I can see that Louis felt that unless I learned to be useful to the party in this way, I would not get much consideration from any of the leaders," Mrs. Roosevelt wrote in her advice book, *You Learn by Living: Eleven Keys for a More Fulfilling Life.*

In August of 1921, FDR was stricken suddenly with polio, a disease which crippled his legs, making them useless. Sara Roosevelt wanted her son to remain at Hyde Park, living out the rest of his days as an invalid. But Louis Howe had other ideas. Together he and Eleanor worked to keep Franklin's spirits up during a long convalescence. In spite of his condition, FDR went on to win both the governorship of New York in 1928 and the presidency of the United States in 1932. But he would never walk again and was confined to a wheel-chair. It was difficult for Franklin to campaign or to travel to see his constituents. On the other hand, his wife was always out and about, meeting and talking with all kinds of people. He became increasingly depen-dent on Eleanor's opinion of political situations.

In the 1920s, Eleanor became more and more involved in politics. She worked closely with the League of Women Voters. In 1928, she headed up the national women's campaign for the Democratic Party. Soon she began expressing her own views on political matters.

Eleanor felt it was her duty as a person born into wealth and prominence to use her position in society to do good. Always an advocate for the poor and weak, she spoke against racial discrimination and for women's rights. Her opinions were considered almost radical by

Franklin and Eleanor at Hyde Park in 1922, less than a year after he contracted polio.   Courtesy of the Franklin D. Roosevelt Library Digital Archives.

the political establishment of the time. FDR, who was a very "practical politician," would frequently apologize for his wife's opinions, saying, "I can't do a thing with her." FDR never tried to quiet Eleanor and while he didn't always agree with her, he always valued her viewpoint on the issues of the day.

❧ Finally, Something of Her Own ❧

In 1924, FDR gave his wife some land next to his Hyde Park estate called Val-Kill. He then had a small, three-bedroom, stone cottage built there to be used as a getaway for Eleanor and "her female political friends." Eventually, Mrs. Roosevelt and her friends Nancy Cook and Marion Dickerman had a furniture factory built on the property and went into business together.

Val-Kill Industries, as the factory was named, was an experimental business. The idea behind it was to provide jobs for young men living in the Hudson Valley. Mrs. Roosevelt and her partners believed that if farm workers learned manufacturing skills, they could better sustain themselves when they couldn't make enough money from farming alone. The women also saw small manufacturing as a way of maintaining the economy in rural areas and keeping rural families from moving away from their farms into already crowded cities.

The Val-Kill factory also promoted traditional American crafts by producing handmade furniture. "We hope to make Val-Kill the center for a revival of all of the old industries which were once carried on in its very hills," said Mrs. Roosevelt. "There is no reason why craftsmanship cannot be restored to American industry," she said in a radio interview. "Let us make the most of the advantages of machinery, I say, but let us also remember that no machine can create beauty in the way that the human hand can create beauty."[20]

Like so many other businesses, Val-Kill Industries fell prey to the Great Depression. People just couldn't afford "luxury" items like handmade furniture. In 1936,

Val-Kill Industries shut down and Mrs. Roosevelt turned the factory into something she had wanted all her life, her own home.

She converted the factory not long after the last group of homesteaders moved into Arthurdale. She spent most of her time in Hyde Park at Val-Kill and after FDR died in 1945, it became her permanent home. From the outside, her home still looked much like a furniture factory. Visiting guests, whether famous or not, were welcomed through a simple back door. Inside, the atmosphere was casual but warm. The wood-paneled walls and wood furnishings were quite similar to those in the Arthurdale homesteads.

Eleanor Roosevelt loved living at Val-Kill. "The greatest thing I have learned is how good it is to come home again," she once told a friend. "My house seems nicer than ever and I could be happy in it alone! That's the last test of one's surroundings."[21]

Mrs. Roosevelt understood the importance of a home because she lived without one for so long. She understood the miners' longing for a place of their own. Perhaps that was why one small West Virginia village was so important to her—for it is doubtful a town called Arthurdale would have existed without her.

CHAPTER 4

In the Nation's Spotlight

"I want you to succeed, not only for yourselves,
but for what it will mean to people everywhere,
North, South, East and West,
who are starting similar projects."

*—Eleanor Roosevelt's address to
Arthurdale's homesteaders, June 1934*

*T*he First Lady's speech was part of a reception at the Arthur Mansion. Along with Arthurdale's "new citizens" the audience consisted of politicians like West Virginia congressman Jennings Randolph; presidential advisers like Louis Howe; wealthy friends of Mrs. Roosevelt like the financier Bernard Baruch; and several members of the press.

❧ *In the News* ❧

It wouldn't be the last time the homesteaders were put on display.   Glenna Williams says the early days of Arthurdale were like "living in a fish bowl."   News reporters and government officials were always around; watching and questioning the homesteaders. On many occasions curious sightseers wandered into the village, further disrupting what little privacy the homesteaders had.

The children of Arthurdale quickly adjusted to all the publicity. "As a kid you didn't notice it so much," says Bob Day. "You were just running around, having fun."   Annabelle Mayor adds, "We didn't resent it as much as we probably should have." Homesteader Luther Zinn says he "kind of enjoyed seeing them." Being curious himself, Zinn frequently stopped and talked with the visitors. But most of the adults felt differently. "Got so a man couldn't set down to his sow belly and turnip greens without some stranger peeking in at the window or walking in to ask some fool questions," growled one frustrated homesteader at the time.[22]

Arthurdale was controversial from the start. Simply being the first government-sponsored homesteading community made it vulnerable to public criticism. Every problem was reported, every decision questioned by the press. And from the beginning there were problems. The first and most notable fiasco involved the community's first fifty houses. FDR's personal secretary and adviser, Louis Howe, had suggested using some prefabricated houses that could be put up quickly. Mrs.

A determined Eleanor defends her experiment to reporters in front of the "under construction" town of Arthurdale. Photo provided by the West Virginia and Regional History Collection, West Virginia University Libraries.

Roosevelt didn't agree and point blank told him, "Louis don't be absurd!"[23] But Howe went and ordered "Cape Cod" style vacation homes anyway. The structures had no insulation and couldn't stand up to a typical Appalachian winter. Worse yet, they didn't even fit the foundations the men of Arthurdale had constructed for them.

Construction stopped while New York architects redesigned the houses for the foundations. The delay was frustrating to Arthurdale's first residents, some of whom were camped out in the cold while waiting for homes. And the cost of "remaking" the houses was widely criticized in the media and even within FDR's administration.

Often when Mrs. Roosevelt was away from the White House, FDR lightheartedly placed the blame for a developing problem on her shoulders. "My missus, unlike most women hasn't any sense about money at all," the president casually told his worried advisers.[24] Sometimes, FDR's easygoing demeanor calmed the nervous people around him. This was not one of those times. Some of those advisers wondered why the homesteaders were "given" so much compared to the rest of the country. After all, in the 1930s, 80 percent of rural America lived without modern conveniences like indoor plumbing and many had nothing to eat.

Harold Ickes, Roosevelt's secretary of the interior, told the president, "The cost of the thing is shocking to me." The cost he was speaking of was more than $10,000 per family. FDR said that was all right "by the fact that it is a model." Ickes wondered what kind of model the president was talking about, "obviously it wasn't a model of low-cost housing."[25]

Eventually the First Lady and Louis Howe made sure Arthurdale families ended up moving into homes with "modern" conveniences like central steam heat, indoor plumbing, and refrigerators. The houses also had built-in bookcases and attractive wood floors. And

This house is a good example of one of the three designs for Arthurdale homes. It was in sharp contrast to what the miners were used to in Scotts Run. Courtesy of the Library of Congress. Edwin Locke, photographer.

because they were built for subsistence farming, the homesteads had pantries, root cellars, smokehouses, and small barns or sheds.

❧ Becoming a Community ❧

Most Arthurdale families found their new homes lavish compared to the shacks in Scotts Run. It was also a big change from the jagged hollows of Monongalia County to the rolling hills of Preston County. Here the houses weren't right on top of each other. People had room for gardens, and fields for growing wheat and raising cows and pigs. Most homesteaders worked clearing about three acres around their property. The food they grew added to their income and their diets. One homesteader wife told the First Lady, "It is paradise for us."[26]

As a planned community, it needed all the things other communities had. But unlike other communities which grow over time, Arthurdale saw that growth and development almost instantaneously. The community needed a school, one was built. It needed a post office, space was found. It needed a store, it got one. Later a restaurant was added to the back of that store. These communal necessities also meant more work and income for homesteader families.

Wood paneling and handmade furniture like these Godlove chairs gave Arthurdale homes a warm atmosphere. Homesteaders made similar furniture in their craft cooperative. Courtesy of the Library of Congress.

The village grew up around the community center. Most of it was built and paid for by government funds under the New Deal legislation. Eleanor Roosevelt also used her influence with many of her wealthy friends to help the homesteaders. Bernard Baruch helped pay salaries of Arthurdale's teachers; he also donated $20,000 to the building of the school and was totally responsible for the construction and outfitting of the high school's gymnasium. The Guggenheims, wealthy industrialists and friends of Baruch, sponsored the building of a dental clinic at Arthurdale. And Dorothy Elmhirst, another wealthy friend of Mrs. Roosevelt, helped finance the infirmary.

"We went to the infirmary if there was anything at all wrong with us," says Luther Zinn. "During the day there was usually a doctor and a nurse there to take care of us." Having adequate health care was a big change for the homesteaders. On Scotts Run, doctors willing to treat poor coal miners were rare.

❧ *Working Together* ❧

The people of Arthurdale took to heart Mrs. Roosevelt's faith in them and her expectation for their community. "You had the feeling you really did have a chance," says Annabelle Mayor.

Edna Day remembers growing up in Arthurdale, "Everyone took pride in their property."

From the very beginning the homesteaders worked hard building their homes, planting their fields, and harvesting the fruits of their labors. Often their children worked alongside them.

"I mowed the grass, kept up with my chores and helped raise the garden," says Bob Day. "I remember picking the raspberries and the strawberries—most of those were canned. We put the apples in the fruit cellar. Then we'd bury the cabbages and dig them up in winter."

Together homesteaders planted orchards of more than 1,500 fruit trees, 5,000 strawberry plants, and 2,000 grapevines.

"Learning to live off the land is the greatest lesson you could teach anybody," says Andrew Wolf who moved to Arthurdale as a young man and appreciated working in his garden all his life.

In 1934, eighty-one homesteaders had produced more than 5,000 gallons of canned vegetables and 1,000 gallons of fruits. Tons of potatoes, squash, pumpkins, cabbages, and root crops like carrots and turnips were harvested.

"I dug potatoes nearly all morning. This afternoon I scrubbed and limed the chicken house. There is lots of hard work here. We have to keep at it all the time," wrote one homesteader in her diary on September 9, 1935.[27]

The food was first used to feed their families; then the surplus was put into a school lunch program. Forty-three families donated their excess crops and seventy-two families volunteered to can food for school lunches.

"We finished the last of the canning for school lunches today," wrote a volunteer for the program. "We have 3,512 quart cans of vegetables. We have 1,000 bushels of potatoes that the men and boys grew and dug. Some days I thought I couldn't spare time to go to the canning kitchen. When I got there I found all the other women. We talked and visited. It was fun."[28]

Joe Roscoe remembers his mother canning 1,000 quarts of vegetables. Annabelle Mayor's mother volunteered her time to cook and serve school lunches. Mayor feels the hard work of their parents was inspiring to

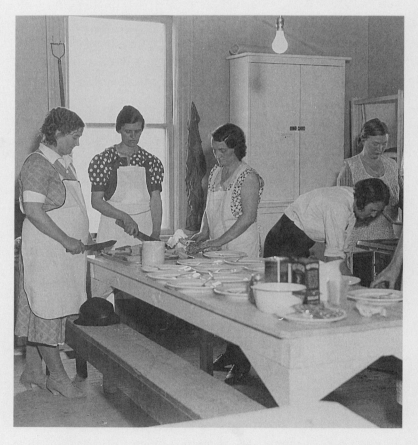

These Arthurdale mothers prepare school lunches for the children. Courtesy of the Library of Congress. Elmer Johnson, photographer.

many of Arthurdale's young people. "Seeing our mothers there cooking and helping meant a lot to us." Even some of the youngest children shared in the experience. "If there was a little one at home, they would just come along with Mom," adds Mayor.

❧ A First Lady and Friend ❧

Few press reports stressed how hard the homesteaders worked or how much their lives had changed since they had moved to Arthurdale. But Mrs. Roosevelt knew. She saw it with her own eyes.

Glenna remembers the First Lady's son, Elliott Roosevelt, saying his mother visited Arthurdale more than any other place during the White House years with the exception of the Roosevelt family home in Hyde Park, New York. "It was a little like 'George Washington slept here'," says Glenna. "Everybody has a story about Mrs. R."

Annabelle Mayor remembers once when Mrs. Roosevelt made a surprise visit to her house. Embarrassed to be seen by the First Lady, Annabelle ran down to the basement. "She had come to see my mother's fruit cellar," says Mayor. The fruit cellar, of course, was in the basement. Mrs. Roosevelt followed Annabelle's mother down the stairs and was pleased with what she saw. After the First Lady left, Annabelle's mother went to look for her. Finding the girl downstairs, she asked her daughter, "Where were you?" Annabelle replied, "Hiding behind the door." Her mother just laughed.

❧ Celebrating Their New Lives ❧

Beyond the hard work, the people of Arthurdale cele-
brated their good fortune. Parties were held. According
to Arthurdale school principal Elsie Clapp, the first
homesteader Christmas was particularly moving:

> A child of one of the families was ill with pneumo-
> nia. Every doctor for miles around was out....I final-
> ly, with the help of the doctor's wife, traced one who
> was out rabbit-hunting. The gathering in the
> crowded hall, packed with all the members of all
> the families, the carols led by a guitar played from
> under the branches of the great tree, the shepherds
> under the stars, the march of the Kings through the
> crowd, the discovery of Mary and the Child bathed
> in light and glory—these were shot through with
> anxiety for the little girl. Finally...came the word
> that the doctor had come and would return again
> later that night. It was, I truly think, in the joys
> and the emotion of that Christmas Eve that the
> spirit of the community was born.[29]

Not all of Arthurdale's Christmases were that emotional but they were still memorable. Mrs. Roosevelt
sent toys for the children. One homesteader remembers
a year when "there was a pair of roller skates in each
box. What fun that was for the kids."[30]

When the First Lady came to visit, there was
always a square dance. "Sixteen hands and circle to the
left. Halfway 'round, chase 'em back. Lady in front, and
gent to her back. Pat your honey on the head; if she

don't like biscuits give her cornbread," the caller yelled into the megaphone, while a group of homesteaders played their fiddles. Mrs. Roosevelt always danced. Bob Day remembers watching her do the Virginia Reel.

Joe Roscoe didn't know how to dance, so he sat outside. "It got so I learned how to dance by watching through the window," says Joe. "Finally some girl invited me inside." Glenna Williams had heard the frequent square dances were an attempt to help the settlers get in touch with their "Scotts-Irish roots." Whatever the reason, the dances and similar events helped unite the people of Arthurdale.

There were also athletic teams and even a community band. Homesteader Henry Donahue played the solo trumpet in the band. The instruments were bought and paid for by the First Lady.

❧ *Trying to Make Good* ❧

Mrs. Roosevelt often told of her positive visits to Arthurdale in a syndicated newspaper column she wrote entitled, "My Day." Other media were not so kind in reporting about the community and many members of Congress criticized the First Lady's "pet project."

At times, as in any community, problems arose with a few residents. Resettlement Administration officials were considering removing five families they thought troublesome until Mrs. Roosevelt intervened. "It seems to me fairly obvious that these people who were taken from Scott's Run could not be expected to be angels," she wrote Rex Tugwell. "The fact that they are making good should be taken into consideration."[31] The fear of being kicked out of Arthurdale if they didn't live up to the government's expectations was real for many homesteaders, as one woman wrote in her diary:

> Tom...is giving his parents trouble and worry. He stole a bicycle and ran away. The county judge paroled him in the custody of the constable in charge of our homesteads. His parents are afraid their homestead may be taken away from them.[32]

But the negative press and occasional problem had little effect on the residents' determination. They wanted to do well for the First Lady's sake. "We pin our faith on Mrs. Roosevelt who has met with us and knows our problems," wrote one homesteader. "We stand with her one hundred percent and naturally criticism of our project is a reflection upon her leadership which is very regrettable."[33]

They also wanted to do well for their own sake. Annabelle Mayor feels many people mistook Arthurdale for a place where "everyone was just taken care of." It was a place where people made decisions about their future and worked together to make that future better. At least that was the way the First Lady saw the project. After one of her many visits, she observed:

> It is true indeed that people can be given opportunities and then throw them away, but it seemed to me as I visited house after house, looking at the faces of the men and women and even the children, that here was determination to keep these small

farms together and make them homes, to take advantage of this opportunity.[34]

Certainly the atmosphere of Arthurdale was a positive influence on the residents, especially the children. "It was cleaner and healthier," says Bob Day. His wife Edna adds, "It was a good place to raise kids—you weren't afraid here."

According to Eleanor Roosevelt, the children from Scotts Run who had once looked so distressed and undernourished now looked "rosy and healthy and supremely happy." Good food and better sanitary conditions could account for most of the improvements. One homesteader wrote in her diary: "Thanksgiving Day was butchering day. We killed our two hogs—they dressed 600 pounds. The men of seven families went together to an old house to do the butchering....We can't be hungry this winter. Jim and I used to pretend we didn't want any meat so the children could have all there was."[35]

It seemed like the youngest children benefited the most by moving to Arthurdale, at least they experienced the quickest transformation.

Glenna was a teenager when her family moved to the homesteader community. For her it was only "a short time before I had to take on more adult responsibilities." One of those responsibilities was working in the nursery. "We had hot lunches for the little ones and mothers came to the nursery school to learn about nutrition," says Glenna. "It was a center for the community with lots of emphasis put on little children."

CHAPTER 5

The Heart of Arthurdale

"It seems you believe in having
the children learn by doing."

*—Homesteader's comment to
Arthurdale's school principal*

*W*hile a hands-on approach to education might not seem that unusual today, it was considered new and strange in the early part of the twentieth century. In the 1920s more schools were built and more children attended classes than ever before but little else changed. Most students memorized facts like their multiplication tables, dates from history, or well-known poems. Then they recited them back to their teachers.

Children of foreign-born citizens and African Americans, like many of the miners on Scotts Run, were considered more suitable for manual labor, and the schools reflected that limited view of their future. Segregation was the law of the land in most places—especially in the South.   Under segregation, African American children went to separate schools from white children.   Although the laws promoting segregation stated schools would be separate but equal, that was far from reality.   Most African Americans attended classes in poorly funded schools equipped with inadequate facilities and outdated textbooks.

By the 1930s, the country's school systems suffered from lack of funds.   Many schools (usually those in the poorest areas) closed.   In some schools that remained open, teachers used their own money to pay for students' supplies and even student lunches.   Perhaps feeling they had little left to lose, many educators began experimenting with new methods of teaching.

One of these pioneers was Elsie Ripley Clapp, the founder, director, and principal of Arthurdale's first school.   Clapp's greatest influence was John Dewey, the educator and philosopher who believed people learn by doing.   For several years, Clapp was Dewey's teaching assistant at Columbia University in New York.   On her application for the job at Arthurdale, Clapp described herself as fifty-four years old; five feet, six inches tall; weighing 147 pounds.   A more accurate description might have been "dynamo in a dress."   She designed Arthurdale's school to help the community and encouraged the community to become involved with the school.   Its success depended upon this shared responsibility.

When the new school opened in the fall of 1934, there were 246 children in grades one through high school.   The school wasn't just the place for children to learn how to read, write, and do arithmetic.   It was the heart of Arthurdale. Homesteaders made the school's desks, blackboards, and other necessities. High school students worked making looms for the community's crafts industry, designed a telephone intercom system between community buildings, and served as assistants in the foundation of Arthurdale's educational program, the nursery, which was like today's preschool.

❧ The Beginnings ❧

Working in the nursery, Glenna Williams saw firsthand the effect living in Arthurdale had on its youngest residents. In 1934, thirty-six children between the ages of three and five were enrolled in the nursery, which started out in the old Arthur mansion and was the only school of its kind in Preston County. The mansion was also the site of the family health clinic.

"If I can teach these mothers that cold pancakes and coffee aren't good for babies," Elsie Clapp told Mrs. Roosevelt, "my two-year-olds will be much healthier."[36] Elsie Clapp did teach the young mothers of Arthurdale about better nutrition. Beginning in 1934, their children had better food, milk, daily doses of cod-liver oil, fresh air, a midday rest, and warmer clothes. Mrs. Roosevelt had purchased snowsuits in various colors and sizes so all the nursery school children could go outside and play in the snow. "They all looked like little birds, all dressed up in those pretty pastel colors," said Mildred Robey, secretary to Arthurdale's project manager and a homesteader herself.

Those simple but essential changes made all the difference in the world. Clapp found the "improvement in the little children physically, mentally, emotionally, and socially through their life and care in a nursery school" almost unbelievable.

That first year, teachers made use of whatever was available. The children played with a few hollow blocks, some packing cases, and sawhorses left over from recent construction.

One nursery school teacher told Elsie Clapp about an imaginative five-year-old named Mathilda. The little girl had placed two sawhorses side by side, hitching some rope from them to blocks made to look like a seat. When the teacher asked her the name of her horses, Mathilda laughed, saying: "That thar one ain't a horse, that's a mule."

Sometimes the children's "make-believing or pretending" reflected the life lived in the mining camps. Mathilda was playing house with five-year old Jack. She told the boy: "You better not work in those mines, Dad. You died there once. You better not do that no more." Jack replied: "It's a lot of work running that machine. If I keep on working in the mines, I'll have a lot of money." Mathilda warned Jack about the danger of the mines but he still told her, "I'm not gonna quit, anyway." Clapp believed that make-believe play brought out "the determination of the male members of the family."[37]

❧ A New Way of Learning ❧

The elementary school also started out in the mansion. The high school and adult education classes were held in the Center building. All began under Elsie Clapp's direction.

Few homesteaders understood her methods but fewer still argued with her success. "It was a new system that Miss Clapp used," said Mildred Robey. "In teaching first graders to read, she'd show them real objects and then have them read the word. I remember one time she brought in a live rabbit. It all seemed kind of silly to me but it seemed to work."

The first grade classroom soon included all of Arthurdale. Instead of staying in the stately old house on the hill, the first graders got on their hats, coats, and boots, and went exploring. They hiked around fields of golden buckwheat planted by the homesteaders. Teacher Ethel Carlisle wrote in her journal on September 17, 1934: "We went over to see the field of buckwheat across the road. We got some of the grains and saw the white substance inside and talked about making flour out of it."[38]

According to Ms. Carlisle, the children were fascinated by "the farm processes" such as planting, plowing, threshing, husking the corn, digging potatoes, milking cows, and making butter with a churn. They also loved tramping through muddy construction sites, watching trucks come and go, and seeing men digging wells. In the spring they saw the laying of the foundation for their new school. It was a huge difference from being stuck in a small miners' shack, or converted schoolroom, similar to their former life on Scotts Run.

The children learned well from this close-up view of Arthurdale's beginnings. It also encouraged them to feel part of the community. The parents liked it too. Mr. Macdonald, a homesteader and father, told the teachers so: "You know, I like the way you people have of having a school—letting the children get out and around, instead of being cooped up all the time. I think it's good."

In 1935, Eunice Jones's second grade class not only learned by watching all the construction around them, they participated by building a child's-size replica of the

Education in Arthurdale encouraged hands-on activities. This class built its own miniature replica of Arthurdale. Courtesy of the Library of Congress.

village of Arthurdale. Jones first talked to her students about where they should build the village. "They all had very sensible ideas about the kind of location they should have—level land," Jones wrote. "And they all wanted shade!" Then the teacher asked: "What should we build first?" Joseph Matthews said: "Put the floors in," and Herndon Bruce said: "Lay the foundation." Second grader Joe Lipton gained confidence watching men building the homesteads. "I see how the roof goes on, now," Joe said. "I think I'll know how to do our roof."[39]

The first fourth grade class at Arthurdale barely had enough paper and pencils for everyone. Yet according to teacher Elisabeth Sheffield, nothing seemed to squash the students' enthusiasm for school. "They loved it," Sheffield wrote in her journal. "The mansion itself was a big, beautiful school to them and with toilets that 'flushed.' I was glad, very glad when I saw how just right it was to them that we had started so simply. Neither the desks, nor the window glass, nor the blackboards matter to them."[40]

Homesteaders provided less traditional school supplies for the fourth grade. John Master dug up some clay from a nearby creek. The students themselves collected corn and ground it between rocks. They also watched flax being threshed when they visited the community's farm. Elisabeth Sheffield wrote her class did "everything we could think of that needed no books or materials."[41] Eventually the fourth grade got desks and blackboards, made by the homesteaders themselves.

❧ *Pioneer Life Comes Alive* ❧

The fourth graders got their family and friends involved in a study of pioneer life. They were encouraged to talk with grandparents and other relatives about their early lives—what it was like cooking over open fires; sleeping in the loft built over one main room; and making most everything that was needed. Homesteaders further helped history come alive by donating old pots, furniture, and some crude tools to the class. Seeing and working with the "ancient treasures" helped the children understand and appreciate their own rich heritage.

Eventually these first fourth graders built a lean-to (sort of like half a log cabin) on one of the trails around Arthurdale. They furnished it with a few primitive antique donations. Whenever they had a break in the school day, they went to the lean-to and reenacted the lives of West Virginia's early settlers.

❧ *Their Own Plays* ❧

Elisabeth Sheffield's second fourth grade class wrote a play about pioneer life and spent a part of each school day rehearsing it at the lean-to. It was a short, dramatic piece set in "the cabin." Some of the children portrayed the settlers and others played friendly Indians who had come for a visit.

The high school drama group also wrote and produced its own plays. Their first effort debuted Thanksgiving Day, 1934, and was about coal mining on Scotts Run. Joe Roscoe acted in it, playing a coal miner injured in a mine accident. By all accounts this early production was a hit in Arthurdale. "Those kids made up that play?" remarked one homesteader in surprise. "Why, I never knew my kids could act. They never was much good in them Sunday school plays down the Run." Another homesteader was also impressed by the performance: "Well, it wasn't half bad, considering that the kids made it up."

Annabelle Mayor remembers participating in another drama group production that also had a pioneer theme. "It was called 'Sweet Betsy from the Pike'," says Annabelle. "About people going west—pioneers I guess. We made our own costumes and everything. Had a natural amphitheater where we performed it." "Sweet Betsy" incorporated traditional songs and ballads into the play:

Did you ever hear tell of sweet Betsy from Pike
Who crossed the wide prairie with her husband Ike?
With two yoke of cattle, an old spotted hog
An old Shanghai rooster and an old yeller dog.

❧ Community Work ❧

As students progressed through the grades, they did more than just learn by watching all the activity around them. They became a vital part of that activity.

The first fifth grade students made a flatboat, a canoe, a fork, a churn, and several looms which were sold or used in Arthurdale's craft shop. Sixth grade shop teacher Harry Carlson was particularly impressed by the work of three of his students who built a trencher table. It was a difficult job but sixth graders Winchell, Dennis, and Justin worked together well. "It combined a great deal of muscular activity with quite a lot of thinking," Carlson said. Another of his students, Martin Dykstra took it upon himself to make use of both tin scraps thrown out by construction workers and the mathematics he had learned in order to design a candle mold.

Sixth grade teacher Katherine Kimble found her class was excited about trying out their new skills and knowledge after school. Mrs. Kimble wrote of two little girls who spent their weekend gathering plants for dyeing fabric, and a little boy who set up a dye-pot at home. The three then experimented with combinations of colors.[42]

"Arthurdale could be studied by an average citizen as a place where all the things he has dreamed of so long for his own community have been put to work," wrote Kimble. "There is much in Arthurdale that other communities could use to their satisfaction: the way the resources of the people are used: the set-up of the community."[43]

The ninth graders made their own mandolins while learning about math and the physics of sound in the process. The best of these was made by a girl whose father was a cabinetmaker. It was displayed at Arthurdale's first music festival held on July 7, 1935. And the eleventh and twelfth graders became responsible for publishing a community newspaper. *The News* announced and reported upon both community and school activities.

Annabelle Mayor remembers an excellent weaving teacher who was born and raised in Sweden. "In school we set up looms and wove material," says Annabelle. "I made a wool suit out of it. Most of those things I wove I still have—three or four dresses and they are still in good condition."

The opportunity to learn new skills while working was much appreciated by boys from the night school classes. A boy named Donald told Harry Carlson, "It seems like before you all came, ther warn't no place in the world for us."

"I like the way this here school's been doing things," homesteader Mr. Macdonald told one teacher. "Course, it may be slower in getting them educated, but it's sure. These kids will know what they know."

❧ *Their New School* ❧

Miss Clapp's and Mrs. Roosevelt's hopes for Arthurdale began with the school. The First Lady often said Arthurdale came to life because of its innovative school and nursery. The school would soon grow and change when it moved into a permanent structure.

Arthurdale's school building was ready for students in the fall of 1935. "The school was used for so many things," remembers homesteader Lova McNair. "When they built the school building, it was like a little community of its own."

Set on the site of a long, sunny meadow, the building was located below the Arthur mansion on the hill. The School Center Building was between the high school and elementary school. In it was the cafeteria and kitchen, the home economics rooms, the community canning

The new and modern Arthurdale High School sits in wide-open land-scape. Courtesy of the Library of Congress. Edwin Locke, photographer.

kitchen, the doctor's offices, the school "bank" and book-store, and the director's office. At the end of the mead-ow in a more secluded area was the nursery school and its playgrounds. Elsie Clapp dubbed it "a little village in itself."

"We really appreciated it," says Annabelle Mayor. "We helped get it ready, by cleaning windows and such. We walked into that brand new building and it was our school."

Most graduates remember it having the "best gym in the county."

Elsie Clapp knew the homesteaders were determined that "the kids should have a better chance." But in spite of the new school, they did not see themselves as changing much. "You ain't never going to make nothing of us," one homesteader told her. "We're like them old apple trees out there, all gnarled and twisted."

At times, Clapp thought the homesteaders had problems getting along and cooperating with each other. "They could not shed a feeling of insecurity and suspicion," she said, "although [they were] deeply stirred by the hope of a new life. Curiously, each was keenly disappointed by this attitude in the others." It was hard for many homesteaders to accept new ideas and approaches. Often they only trusted in their "old ways." Speaking to Fletcher Collins, the teacher for seventh and eighth graders, one homesteader said of his son: "He's a bit contrary, and you'll have to look out for him playing hooky. If he runs away, or doesn't get his lessons good, I want you just to whip him good—just give him a good whipping."

Glenna Williams also saw a regression with children who were absent from the nursery school for any length of time. "Often they drifted back into the old patterns [of bad nutrition]," Glenna says. "It was hard to change their ways and some had difficulty adjusting."

As the construction waned and the homesteaders got more settled, many worried how their children would fare in the outside world with such an "unusual" education.

In 1936 Elsie Ripley Clapp left Arthurdale. The community's school then came under the control of the Preston County School Board. Rexford G. Tugwell, presidential advisor and head of the Resettlement Administration, was one of many disappointed with the change:

"The morale at Arthurdale and conditions there were 90 percent better than in any other homestead, entirely due to the school."[44]

Some of Clapp's ideas lingered, but by 1940 Arthurdale's school was not any different from any other public school in the United States.

CHAPTER 6

A Victim of the Times

"Can you tell me when the factory will be started?
I get panicky every now and then about
these people having work."

—*Eleanor Roosevelt in a letter to Oscar Chapman of
the Department of the Interior, November 1934*

As long as the homesteaders were busy building their community, they could earn enough money to pay their monthly bills including their house payments. For this, the average homestead family needed an annual income of $1,000. There was a hopeful and buoyant atmosphere in the midst of all the activity and new construction. "I think sometimes the people in the surrounding areas were jealous of us," says Annabelle Mayor. "That only strengthened our determination to make our community work."

Arthurdale was supposed to become more self-suffi-
cient over time. Its residents would rely less on wages
from government work and more on income from small
industries and businesses attracted to the village. The
newness and the excitement of the experience began to
wear off as the reality of the times set in. With businesses struggling to survive in urban areas, it was unlikely one would go through the expense of moving to a
more isolated rural area. Scotts Run miners and their
families had moved to Arthurdale to escape some of the
worst poverty of the Great Depression only to find their
new community another victim of the times.

❧ Politics and Publicity ❧

The first attempt to locate employment for the homesteaders began as early as October 1933. Louis Howe
proposed a factory be built in Arthurdale with funds
from the Public Works Administration. The plant would
make wooden furniture and wooden lock boxes for the
U.S. Post Office.

But Howe's plan hit a snag before it was even considered by Congress. Several congressmen complained
that an Arthurdale plant would take jobs away from
their constituents. The fiercest charge came from
Indiana congressman Louis Ludlow. The Keyless Lock
Company in Indianapolis, Indiana was in Ludlow's congressional district. It also made and sold Post Office
equipment. Ludlow wrote President Roosevelt: "I cannot believe this policy has your sanction."[45]

Once shy and self-conscious, Eleanor Roosevelt quickly learned to play the game of politics. Here she addresses the public at Arthurdale in 1933. Courtesy of the Franklin D. Roosevelt Library Digital Archives.

Congressmen Daniel Reed of New York wondered why the administration supported a factory in Arthurdale when more than three thousand men waited for government-sponsored jobs in Jamestown, New York, a town known for its furniture-making.

One of the few openly supportive people for the factory was Silliman Evans, fourth Assistant Postmaster General. Evans felt such a plant would eventually "develop incontrovertible facts" that Keyless and similar companies were simply charging the government too much for what they made. Evans felt that the Arthurdale factory might break the monopoly held by the Post Office suppliers. Despite Evans's support, congressional opposition prevailed. No such factory would be built in the homesteading community.

While Congress thwarted every effort to find employment for the homesteaders, the news media continued to criticize the First Lady's "pet project" as an exercise in the radical politics of the day. And in many ways the Arthurdale project was radical—after all, nothing quite like it had ever been done before by the federal government.

FDR had grown unpopular with many rich and powerful people because his social policies challenged their authority. Many of those policies were judged to be too closely aligned with Communism, a system of government that stresses the importance of economic equality over individual freedom. Mrs. Roosevelt was a major proponent of those social policies and an outspoken, independent woman. That made her an easy target for criticism.

Critics described Arthurdale as a "communist plot" even though the community was started in part to ward off such a "revolution" in the coalfields. Criticism came from all parts of the country. William A. Wirt, a school superintendent in Gary, Indiana, accused Mrs. Roosevelt of being part of a communist "brain trust" and called Arthurdale a "communistic project" which ruined northern West Virginia's tax and rent base when two hundred families relocated to the homesteading community.

"I hardly think it would be found that people on relief were paying much, if any rent," the First Lady responded to the charges. "I do not understand how he considers it Communistic to give people a chance to earn their own living and to buy their own houses. It is a fact that the Government will provide the initial capital, but I hope that many private enterprises will do it throughout the country in the future."[46] Despite the defense of Mrs. Roosevelt, many continued to think of Arthurdale as nothing more than an expensive, radical experiment in direct opposition to American political values.

❧ Looking in the Private Sector ❧

After politics and negative publicity killed the possibility of a government-sponsored factory being built at Arthurdale, Mrs. Roosevelt and Louis Howe looked for an industry from the private sector. By July 1934, Howe found the Electric Vacuum Cleaner Company of Cleveland, Ohio interested in the homesteading community. Howe worked with Julius Tuteur, president of the company, to develop a plan for a factory. The Arthurdale Association, the homesteaders' corporation, would build the factory with monies from the Subsistence Homesteads Corporation, a government program. Some of the

This homesteader assembles vacuum cleaner parts in one of the factories at Arthurdale. Courtesy of the Library of Congress. Ben Shahn,
photographer.

monies would be paid back by the homesteaders themselves. Then the vacuum cleaner company would lease
the factory from the homesteaders for ten to fifteen
years for their operation. The company could cancel their
lease if for some reason they had to stop production.

By July 1935 the factory was up and ready to employ forty to fifty homesteaders. But because of certain
legal problems, operations didn't start until the spring of
1936. There were never more than thirty people em-
ployed at the plant. Tuteur said not enough people were
buying the specific vacuum cleaner models produced at
Arthurdale. The vacuum cleaner company wanted and

needed government contracts to keep their Arthurdale operation going. Tuteur's son John wrote in a letter to Washington officials: "If we could get all the government vacuum cleaner business, based upon the same quantities purchased by them last year, it would give us approximately six weeks operation in Reedsville (Arthurdale), on this business alone." Government officials promised their support. One told Tuteur he would do "everything I possibly can to promote the purchase of your product by various government agencies." In 1937 Tuteur closed the factory for new model changes. He promised the situation was only temporary but as vacuum cleaner sales continued to drop, Arthurdale's plant remained closed.[47]

"When the vacuum cleaner company fell down on their promise to us, it weakened our structure more than I can tell you," Allie Freed told the First Lady. "But I suppose we all have to take our blows with a smile."[48] A good friend of Mrs. Roosevelt, Freed had taken it upon himself to find jobs for the people of Arthurdale. In February 1937, Freed convinced the Phillips-Jones Shirt Company—makers of Van Heusen shirts and other apparel—to move into another factory built in the homesteading community and employ twenty to twenty-five women.

Freed hoped the shirt factory would not only change the community's economic outlook but its public image as well. "I believe that if we provide a continuity of honest news based upon a sound, business-like foundation, it will not be very long before the 'knockers,' both in and out of the government, will have to find a better hunting ground than Arthurdale," he told the First Lady.[49] Mrs. Roosevelt responded by telling Freed to order the first dozen shirts made for President Roosevelt. In June 1937, thirty-four women began working at the factory; operations slowed to a halt by October of that year. They resumed again in March of 1938; but by August of that year, the shirt factory, like the vacuum cleaner factory, shut down, never to reopen. Once again hard economic times stalled the need for the factory's goods.

A series of businesspeople—many of them promoting impractical and often bizarre ideas—showed interest in the homesteading community. A California scientist wanted to make air-conditioned clothes in Arthurdale. A Pennsylvanian suggested a factory to develop "practice bombs." And a man from Hyde Park, New York wanted the government to help him produce "Clopin"—a pill made from cod-liver oil. The Food and Drug Administration found it took 24 capsules of "Clopin" to provide the amount of vitamin D in a single dose of cod-liver oil.

In 1938 the homesteaders' association borrowed $325,000 from the Farm Security Administration to build and equip a factory to make farm tractors. After only sixteen months, the tractor factory also shut down.

In spite of the difficulty recruiting industry, Annabelle Mayor remembers, "There was more employment in Arthurdale than in [nearby] Reedsville and Masontown put together." More than half of those jobs were government jobs. Many homesteaders learned new skills while working in the village's craft and agricultural cooperatives.

❦ Cooperation and Dependency ❦

"Everybody shared; that was what made the community," said homesteader Bertie Swick. From the beginning, Arthurdale's homesteaders were encouraged to come together and create working cooperatives. The cooperatives provided jobs for them and services to their community. Within no time at all, the village had a cooperative health clinic, a cooperative barbershop, and a cooperative store. Luther Zinn's wife worked in the store. "For a country store it was a pretty good store," said Zinn. When the restaurant was added in the back of the store, Zinn's wife became the restaurant manager.

One cooperative had particularly close ties to the First Lady. In the 1920s, Mrs. Roosevelt had her own small furniture-making company on the grounds of Val-Kill, the home FDR had built for her on property connected to their Hyde Park, New York estate. She brought in her friend and business partner, Nancy Cook, to develop a furniture-making program in Arthurdale. The furniture-making co-op became part of the Arthurdale branch of the Mountaineer Craftsmen's Cooperative. The First Lady was verbally attacked for her interest in the furniture cooperative. Minnesota Senator Thomas called the president's wife "a price-gouging publicity hound." In defense of the Arthurdale cooperative and her own factory, Mrs. Roosevelt said they were doing more than just making furniture and providing jobs, they were making "made-to-order works of art." She went on to say, "I would like to explain that our factory at Val-Kill was started [in 1925] as an experiment to see if one could run a very small factory in a

| CO-OP STORE |

Arthurdale, W. Va.

Are you Patronizing your Co-op Store?
Greater Volume Means Greater Savings.
Remember it is Your Store.

PRICES EFFECTIVE WEEK NOVENBER 7 to 4

CANNED GOODS

Libbys Pumpkin	Lg. can	15cts.
Pancake Syrup	12 oz.Bottle	10cts.
	Rumford	
Baking Powder 6oz. cans 12cts.	12oz. cans	22cts.
Houoe of Lords TEA Quarter lb. Pkg.		22cts.

COFFEE

French Drip	3lb. for 47 cts'
Break O Morn	lb. 19cts·
Show Boat	lb. 23cts.

Cereal

Shreeded Wheat	2 for 23cts.
Kelloggs All-Bran	2Pks. 23cts.

Glass Measuring Cup

Free

With Each Purchase

Cream of Wheat 14oz.Pkg.	13cts.
Mothers Oats Reg. Pkg.	9cts.

Flour

Pillsbury Best	$1.13
Town Crier	$1.13
Buckwheat Flour	5lb. 25cts.
10lb.	45cts.

SPECIAL ITEMS

Bathroom Paper		
Northern Tissue	4 Rolls	25cts.
Gauze	3Rolls	13cts.
Uneeda Biscuits 2 Pkg.		9cts.
Wax Paper	2 Rolls	15cts.
Avoid Coffee Nerves		
PostumCerealPkg.		23cts.

Soap

P&G	6 for25cts.
Octagon Laundry	6 for25cts.
Camay Toilet	5cts.
Palm Olive	2 for 11cts.
Ivory	Lg. 2 for19 Med. 2 for 11

The co-op store encouraged Arthurdale residents to support it by offering weekly sales. This flier advertises many name brands that are still available today. Courtesy of Arthurdale Heritage, Inc.

rural community and make it pay and at the same time teach people—boys especially—a trade so that they would not drift out of the country community. We have never, since we began, any of us who put the money into the factory, had one cent of interest in our investment."[50]

The chairs made in Arthurdale were indeed thought of as "works of art." To insure high quality craftsmanship, master chairmaker Bud Godlove was brought in to train Arthurdale workers. "Mr. Godlove was an old mountaineer who passed down to us the art of making chairs," recalls homesteader Henry Donahue. The "Godlove chairs," as they came to be known, were simple double-caned, ladder-back chairs made from native hickory and walnut. "That furniture was beautiful, hand rubbed," says homesteader Mildred Robey. "Apparently they sold for big prices in New York City."

Other crafts produced in the cooperative included metalwork in pewter, copper, and iron, as well as knitted goods and weavings. "We put our hearts into it and made beautiful things," says Annabelle Mayor, who wove many different items, including a candlewick bedspread.

Homesteader Lova McNair has always been interested in art. She learned how to make pottery on a potter's wheel. She made vases, mugs, cups, even a whole tea set. She also learned how to weave. Before long she bought her own loom for $25. "A boy in the woodworking shop had made one for his mother and I asked him to make one for me," says Lova. Eventually she joined Arthurdale's branch of the Mountaineer Craftsmen and sold her work.

Both McNair and Mayor were encouraged to ask a good price for their work. But even many homesteaders thought the prices for the handcrafted items were too high. By 1936, furniture worth $43,000 was sold from the Arthurdale cooperative. However most handcrafted items had become luxuries during the Depression. Few people had the extra money to buy the high quality, specially made goods like the Godlove chair.

❧ On West Virginia's Homefront ❧

As World War II came on in the late 1930s, even before American troops were deployed to fight in Europe and the Pacific, the United States supported the war efforts of England and France. That support meant more work for the homesteaders in and out of Arthurdale as factories geared up to produce tanks, fighter jets, and other weapons. Many men returned to work in the coal mines. When the U.S. entered the war in 1941, a number of young men from Arthurdale enlisted. "When the war came about one tenth of the population was in the service," says Bob Day. "There were at least 100 boys from Preston County; more than most other [West Virginia] counties."

Some industry did move into the community. In April 1940, the Silman Manufacturing Company moved into the tractor factory. Nearly one hundred women worked there making walkie-talkies, public address equipment, and flares. At about the same time the Brunswick Radio and Television Company set up shop to manufacture cabinetry, radios, record players, and speakers. Within Brunswick's first five months of operation, it sold more than $250,000 worth of goods and paid out $50,000 in wages.

On June 11, 1940, Harry Johnson of the Arthurdale Veterans Committee wrote to Major J.O. Walker of the

Resettlement Administration, "Our greatest handicap as a community has been the uncertainty of future employment." The committee was asking for "some sort of industry in connection with the National Defense Program" to fill Arthurdale's dormant factories. In 1943 Arthurdale finally landed that major defense contractor. Hoover Aircraft Corporation, which made wooden simulated airplanes used for training pilots, took over all of Arthurdale's factories—including the Silman Manufacturing Company and the Brunswick Radio and Television Company plants.

With the advent of World War II, America's bleak economic picture turned around. There were jobs again and the prosperity continued after the war ended. This era was also the time when the government prepared to pull out of the homesteading village, a move that would eventually make Arthurdale a pleasant bedroom community without an economic base of industry.

While she never gave up on the homesteaders, Eleanor Roosevelt came to agree with many economists and government officials of the time. Instead of building a community and looking for industry to provide jobs, it was better if industry found a location first, and "then the community grows around it."

CHAPTER 7

The First Lady Stands by the Homesteaders

"Nothing we learn in this world is ever wasted and
practically nothing we do ever stands by itself.
If it is good, it will serve some good purpose
in the future. If it is evil, it may haunt and
handicap our efforts in unimagined ways."

—*Eleanor Roosevelt*, This I Remember, *1949*

*A*fter Arthurdale's 1942 commencement, Mrs. Roosevelt remarked, "The twenty fine looking young people who received their diplomas yesterday show great progress."[51] Yet even as she spoke the government was beginning the long process of pulling its support from the homesteading community.

❧ The Government Abandons the Homesteaders ❧

Arthurdale's children, and their parents, had already experienced the transition from government-sponsored, community run schools to becoming part of the Preston County School System in 1936. With that change came the reorganization of several cooperatives, including the health and baby clinics. The Homesteaders Club took over running the music festivals and athletics, like the baseball team. At that time, Mrs. Roosevelt encouraged the homesteaders to carry on and make their experimental community work. On July 12, 1936, she wrote a letter to Bernard Baruch: "I stressed to them that I was not in anyway lessening my interest and would be there as often as I had been in the past." And of course, she kept her word.

But by 1941, when the United States entered World War II, Arthurdale had become a political problem for the Roosevelt Administration. The country's focus had changed from helping those struck down by Depression-era poverty to gearing up for war across both the Atlantic and Pacific Oceans.

"Sell it off—regardless" was the unspoken motto of the National Housing Authority, which took over the task of ridding the government of its financial interests in Arthurdale.

The first experimental homesteading community cost the government approximately 2 million dollars, a small amount considering modern federal government budgets. In 1946, the government sold the community's 165 houses; most were bought by the homesteaders themselves. The hillside inn, forge, weaving room, furniture-display room, and the 57,250 square feet of factory space were sold to outside interests. By 1948, the government's fourteen-year involvement with Arthurdale ended. During those years the homesteaders' only constant source of support was the First Lady.

"She had a heart of gold," says homesteader Mildred Robey of Mrs. Roosevelt. "She saw the misery, had a vision and wanted to help her fellow man. I loved that woman. If ever anyone went to heaven I'm sure she did."

But all the First Lady's goodwill could not stop the inevitable. It was time for Arthurdale to stand on its own and be just like any other community.

Homesteader opinions on the government pulling out were varied.

"I think the government was very patient," says homesteader Luther Zinn. "We had a chance to better ourselves; some wanted everything given to them, and time weeded those people out."

But Zinn did acknowledge that it was tough on some people.

"It was sad to see it go," says homesteader Beulah Myers. Glenna Williams thinks the community lost a "sense of unity" when it was no longer a homestead: "It just became another collection of homes in West Virginia."

❧ *Dependency on Mrs. R.* ❧

The First Lady's support was both a blessing and a curse to the homesteading community. When a reporter asked Mrs. Roosevelt why she went to Arthurdale so often, she replied she enjoyed the homesteaders' company. And by all accounts, she did.

The homesteaders felt they knew her. M. L. Wilson, head of the Subsistence Homestead Division, said Mrs. Roosevelt had a "folksy and home-like way with the homesteaders as though she had always lived in the community and had just come back from having been gone for a couple of weeks."[52]

Mildred Robey recalls the First Lady being in a meeting with homesteaders: "She was just knitting like crazy. The needles just kept going 'click, click, click' and she never even had to look at what she was doing."

She square-danced with them, discussed the news of the day with them, and visited the homes with sick children and those with newborn babies. Homesteader Beulah Myers remembers one such visit: "She was so amazed I was up doing laundry and making bread [after giving birth]."

Mrs. Roosevelt comforted them in difficult times—especially during World War II. "She came to the house, put her arms around me and told me 'you have a son missing in action'," says homesteader Annabelle Davis. Davis further recalls that when the First Lady returned to Washington, she sent her a telegram letting her know her son was in a German prisoner of war camp. "Every time she came back to Arthurdale she told me how he was getting along," says Davis.

"Mrs. R.," as many called her, would also visit homesteaders for no particular reason. On a visit to Bertie Swick's house, Bertie overheard the First Lady comment on her housekeeping. "She must not have any children," Mrs. Roosevelt said pointing. "No treadmarks on the walls."

The First Lady became more than a friend to the homesteaders. She was their "angel," the one they turned to when anything went wrong. Whenever something needed to be done, the homesteaders could count on "Mrs. R." to cut through the red tape. But there were times they depended too much on her help and not enough on their own resources. Once when their school bus broke down, the homesteaders actually sent it to the White House garage for repairs. Later Mrs. Roosevelt confided in her friend and biographer, Joseph P. Lash, her disappointment in the homesteaders' lack of initiative: "They seemed to feel the solution to all their problems was to turn to government."[53]

Mrs. Roosevelt never considered Arthurdale a charity but a social experiment. And while she knew sometimes, "charity may be necessary, our aim should be to get people back to a point where they can look after themselves. I have never felt that people should be grateful for charity. They should rightfully be resentful and so should we, at the circumstances which make charity a necessity."[54]

❧ *Frustrations over Arthurdale* ❧

The fact that the homesteaders went to the First Lady with their problems frustrated many administration officials, whose job it was to oversee the resettlement of the community. Both Harold Ickes and Rex Tugwell

suffered from lack of direct contact with the homesteaders. In his diary, Ickes called Arthurdale, "just one big
headache from the beginning." They felt pressure to not
disagree with Mrs. Roosevelt. After all, she was their
boss's wife, and to further complicate matters, she often
tempered her requests in such a way as to make them
hard to refuse. When the First Lady complained about
pay cuts to the homesteader construction workers, she
approached Tugwell with, "I hope you will not think me
an interfering old hen."[55] It is safe to say that, at times,
Tugwell thought she was just that.

There were times too, when the First Lady became
frustrated with the homesteaders. She realized they were
put into a totally new situation in the beginning and that
they had "to learn to stand on their own feet and make
their own decisions." But she admitted that "sometimes
they didn't quite know what was expected of them." And
other times, she couldn't understand why they hung on to
their old ways. "They wanted cows tied to their back
fences," Mrs. Roosevelt said in later years. "They trusted
nobody, not even themselves. They had an eye out all the
time to see who was going to cheat them next."[56]

Still the First Lady admired all that the homesteaders had accomplished and she believed in encour-
aging, rather than criticizing them. This was especially
the case for Arthurdale's young people.

Mrs. Roosevelt was at every high school graduation
at Arthurdale. She signed all the diplomas, and usually
she was the keynote speaker. Despite the status of her
position, she impressed the homesteaders and their children with her down-to-earth nature. Bob Day was the
president of his senior class, and a bit on the short side

for his age. As class president, one of his jobs was to pin a corsage on the tall First Lady. "She said to someone, 'Oh, he's not old enough!' to be graduating," says Bob. "But she was a grand lady; could talk to you about anything."

Her personal interest in Arthurdale's success influenced others to help the community—people like Bernard Baruch and tobacco heiress Doris Duke. And in 1938, it even brought the president himself to speak at Arthurdale's high school graduation ceremonies.

❧ *A Presidential Visit* ❧

Annabelle Mayor was all set to graduate high school in 1938. She even had an important part in the commencement program. She was to step up to the podium, make a little speech, and then give some flowers to First Lady Eleanor Roosevelt.

Shortly before school ended, the principal called her into his office. The principal asked if Annabelle would do a favor for the school, because there would be a special guest at graduation. "I gave up my part in the program for the president," says Annabelle. "I was glad to do it." Later Annabelle and her classmates were invited to the White House. "Never in my wildest dreams, did I think I would visit the White House; and there I was, in the private dining room, having lunch."

The day the president arrived for the 1938 commencement ceremonies was very busy. "There were people everywhere," says Annabelle. Mildred Robey made her house available to FDR—who needed a wheelchair because his bout with polio had made his legs useless. "My home was on level ground and easy for him to move in and out of," says Mildred. "Oh, he was a fine looking, handsome man; I remember talking to him on the phone when he'd call for Mrs. Roosevelt—he had a beautiful voice."

Even though most reporters were aware of FDR's condition, the general policy of the press at the time was to show the president as strong physically. He was almost never photographed in his wheelchair. Lights in the auditorium were turned off until he was brought on stage for his speech.

In this 1938 photo, FDR enjoys a moment with Arthurdale High School graduates after making his commencement address to the class. Photo provided by West Virginia and Regional History Collection, West Virginia University Libraries.

"These projects represent something new," President Roosevelt said of the homesteading communities in his Arthurdale graduation address. He called Arthurdale a "bold government venture,"—one in which lessons could be learned for future generations. He said these lessons would save "a hundred times their cost in dollars."

Despite Arthurdale's problems, it was a wonderful place to live: a close-knit community in which people supported each other, and one in which industrial decay was exchanged for healthy, country living. In many ways, it was an excellent example of how to plan a town or village. But Arthurdale never overcame early criticism or the politics of the time, and therefore few, if any, learned from its lessons.

By 1942, the experiment was over—Arthurdale was no longer a resettlement community. It was just a town like any other in West Virginia.

CHAPTER 8

Arthurdale's Legacy

"It is a story that shouldn't die."

—*Glenna Williams*

*A*t first glance Arthurdale today doesn't
seem to have changed much since the 1930s. A couple of
cows graze alongside white sheds; they are joined by
some goats, and even a few ducks. The small homes,
some still painted a cheerful white, dot the gently, rolling
hills of grass on this mountain plateau. There are well-
kept gardens in many yards.

The Center complex, the administration building,
and the forge still stand just off route 92. Across the road,
the tract of white structures that once housed Arthurdale's nursery, elementary, and high schools is hidden
behind the new Valley Elementary School. The old Arthur
mansion no longer stands in the background—part of it

burned down in the 1940s and soon after, the rest was torn down.

The clatter of construction has long since died down; the crowds of visiting press people and those trying to catch a glimpse of famous politicians and their famous wives no longer come here. The only cooperative operating now is Arthurdale's cemetery. But neighbors still drop in on neighbors. The Center building is still a place for square dancing, as well as parties for young people. Families with young children live alongside many of the original homesteaders. Today, Arthurdale is a quieter, calmer place—a nice place to live and bring up children.

Glenna Williams, Annabelle Mayor, and Bob Day and his wife Edna still live here, along with the homesteaders' descendents. Many of those descendents have moved back to the area, lured here by fond memories of the past and the promise of professional jobs in nearby Morgantown and Fairmont.

❦ *Arthurdale's Descendents* ❦

"I have always felt that many human beings who might have cost us thousands of dollars in tuberculosis sanitariums, insane asylums, and jails were restored to usefulness and given confidence in themselves," wrote Eleanor Roosevelt of the Arthurdale experiment.[57] She was referring to the effects the devastating poverty and deplorable living conditions of Scotts Run could have had on future generations now living at Arthurdale.

The homesteaders were lucky; lucky to have moved from the crowded and unsanitary conditions of the Scotts Run coal camps; lucky to have been part of an experimental community supported by a generous First Lady; lucky to have been able to build, and eventually pay for, their own homes; even lucky that all the young men who volunteered for the service during World War II returned home to Preston County. The homesteaders appreciated their luck and they made the most of the opportunities afforded them.

Their children benefited even more, from their parents' good fortune and their hard work. Almost all went on to college: becoming teachers, doctors, lawyers, artists, musicians, accountants, librarians, and historians. Past and present Arthurdale residents are proud of their unique history. They manage to preserve it through the nonprofit organization, Arthurdale Heritage, Inc. Jennifer Bonnette is the granddaughter of the oldest living homesteader couple, Claude and Hazel Bonnette. Along with Deanna Hornyak, the executive director of Arthurdale Heritage, Inc., she operates the small museum in the administration building. Deanna's husband, Robert, is another homesteader descendent who moved back to the area.

Like their parents and grandparents, those who have chosen to return to Arthurdale support the community. Most of the donations to the museum come from the homesteaders, their children, and their grandchildren. "We operate on fairly small donations; we really celebrate when someone gives us $500," says Deanna. "But people are fairly constant with their giving; they support us."

❧ *The Past Meets the Present* ❧

Kenny Kidd greets visitors to his homestead house as if they were officials from Washington, D.C. inspecting the Arthurdale project. His home is one of the original homesteads. Dressed in simple clothes from the 1930s, Kidd tells the group his wife is gone for the day but "they are welcome to come in and look around."

Kidd is actually an unmarried graduate student from nearby West Virginia University. The visitors are no more official than any other tourists wandering through Preston County. Kidd's role-playing brings the tour group back in time, as they enter the fully restored homestead. They are shown white cabinets in the kitchen, warm wood floors, and a fireplace flanked by small bookcases and Godlove chairs in the living room. Upstairs are four modestly furnished bedrooms, only two are open to the public, and a small tiled bathroom. It is a pretty little house, one any homesteader would be proud of, and Kidd enjoys telling the story of Arthurdale.

Homesteaders and their descendents always celebrate Arthurdale's anniversary the first weekend in July. What started out as a "multi-family reunion" has turned into Preston County's popular "New Deal" festival. "We wanted it to have a broader appeal," says Jennifer Bonnette. "We bring in local artisans, crafters, blacksmiths, and weavers, and if you're lucky, you might even catch a glimpse of Eleanor Roosevelt." An actor plays the part of the First Lady while some of the children of original homesteaders celebrate their school class reunions. Many wear T-shirts that read: "Arthurdale/The Dream Lives On." It is important for the

What for years had been a get-together much like a large family reunion has now become the New Deal Festival. Held every Fourth of July weekend in Arthurdale, it attracts visitors from all over. Courtesy of Arthurdale Heritage, Inc.

homesteaders to remember. They enjoy talking about the past, recalling how their unique opportunity has shaped their lives and the lives of their children.

❧ *Success or Failure?* ❧

From the first, Arthurdale was an experiment in making a successful community. First Lady Eleanor Roosevelt risked tremendous criticism to continue what she and others started. Many considered Arthurdale nothing more than another "giveaway" program created by FDR's New Deal legislation. The seeds of today's welfare programs were planted in the Roosevelt administration of the 1930s. Aid to Dependent Families began in 1935 as an effort to help young widows stay home with their small children. Other government-funded welfare programs were passed into law during the 1950s and 1960s. But Arthurdale wasn't a program that just gave money away to individuals; instead it brought individuals together to build a new community. And in that respect Arthurdale was successful.

Arthurdale's failure to support itself by bringing in local industry is offset by the rich community life it brought the homesteaders. The way in which the village was planned—allowing for both farm and town life to thrive—is a lesson in community development. Answering critics in September 1934, Eleanor Roosevelt wrote, if the experiment of Arthurdale wasn't worth doing, then "we must go along the beaten path and be contented with the same type of living which has driven people out of rural districts in the past and into the cities where they have become equally unhappy under present industrial conditions."[58]

In contrast to Arthurdale, those who live along Scotts Run today still contend with difficult living and working conditions and a poorer standard of living.

As the first resettlement community, Arthurdale paved the way for about one hundred other such communities across the country: some on the East Coast, like Aberdeen Gardens, outside of Norfolk, Virginia; some out in the western United States, like Three

Rivers, Texas; and a few more in Appalachian coal country, like Eleanor, West Virginia, named after the First Lady. None of the resettlement communities that followed Arthurdale had the assistance or attention of First Lady Eleanor Roosevelt. Each developed in its own unique way. Aberdeen Gardens' residents were African American workers, many of whom had been laid off from jobs in the shipbuilding industry. As a "garden community," it was much more urban in nature than Arthurdale.

It is doubtful the government today would support a project like Arthurdale. The economic cost would simply be too high. Still, the idea of homesteading has a lot in common with one successful nonprofit organization, Habitat for Humanity. Habitat provides a way for people to work for the home built for them; a way for them to keep their dignity, while being given a chance to do better economically. Many of Arthurdale's residents recognize the similarity. "I have often thought the reason so many here give to Habitat is because they truly understand all that owning your own home means," says Glenna Williams.

Even though the original houses were criticized for being inadequate structures, they have stood the test of time and the wear of many bitter Appalachian winters. They have also held their value. In general, homesteader houses are priced, and sell, for about twice that of similar real estate in Preston County. "They get a good price," said Glenna Williams in 1999. "One small homestead just sold for $92,000."

But the real legacy of Arthurdale is its people. Because they were given some hope in desperate times, they have chosen to help others. Because they had a First Lady believe in them and in their future, they have provided their children, and their children's children, with a brighter future. Because they worked hard and learned, they can be proud of all they accomplished, with a little help from the New Deal.

NOTES

1. I. C. White, "Morgantown's Wealth of Fuel," *Black Diamond* 71 (11 August 1923): 178-79.

2. Sidney D. Lee, *"And the Trees Cried"* (Morgantown, W.Va.: Sidney D. Lee, 1991). 22.

3. March 13, 1935 entry in Mary Behner's journal published in "I Wonder Whom God Will Hold Responsible" *West Virginia History* 53 (1994): 83.

4. Lee, *"And the Trees Cried,"* 33.

5. Bryan Ward, ed., *A New Deal for America: Proceedings from a National Conference on New Deal Communities* (Arthurdale, W.Va.: Arthurdale Heritage, Inc., 1995). 12.

6. Ibid., 12.

7. Eleanor Roosevelt, *This I Remember* (New York: Harper & Brothers, 1949). 128.

8. Joseph P. Lash, *Eleanor and Franklin: The Story of Their Relationship Based on Eleanor Roosevelt's Private Papers* (New York: W.W. Norton & Company, Inc., 1971). 393-94.

9. Ibid., 395.

10. Blanche Wiesen Cook, *Eleanor Roosevelt: Volume Two, 1933-1938* (New York: Viking, 1999). 138

11. Ibid., 139.

12. Lash, *Eleanor and Franklin,* 33.

13. Ibid., 61.

14. Russell Freedman, *Eleanor Roosevelt: A Life of Discovery* (New York: Clarion Books, 1993). 24.

15. All quotes from Lash, *Eleanor and Franklin,* 87.

16. Ibid., 87.

17. Russell Freedman, *Eleanor Roosevelt,* 33-34.

18. Blanche Wiesen Cook, *Eleanor Roosevelt: Volume One, 1884-1933* (New York: Viking Penguin, 1992). 391.

19. Cook, *Eleanor Roosevelt: Volume One,* 109.

20. Cook, *Eleanor Roosevelt: Volume Two,* 147.

21. Freedman, *Eleanor Roosevelt,* 185.

22. Ward, *A New Deal for America,* 82.

23. Cook, *Eleanor Roosevelt: Volume Two,* 135-36.

24. Ibid.

25. Ibid.

26. Ward, *A New Deal for America,* 89.

27. "Monthly Narrative Report, Sept. 25, 1937." RG 96, National Archives.

28. T.R. Pharr to Glenn Work memorandum, 9 July 1938. Eleanor Roosevelt Papers, series 70, Franklin D. Roosevelt Library, Hyde Park, N.Y.

29. Elsie Ripley Clapp, *Community Schools in Action* (New York: Viking Press, 1939). 103.

30. Cook, *Eleanor Roosevelt: Volume Two,* 142.

31. Stephen Edward Haid, "Arthurdale: An Experiment in Community Planning, 1933-1947" (Ph.D. diss., West Virginia University, 1975), 207-8.

32. Ibid., 208.

33. Ibid., 95.

34. Ward, *A New Deal for America,* 89.

35. "Diary of a Homesteader's Wife," *Liberty* (2 January 1937): 12.

36. Clapp, *Community Schools in Action,* 93.

37. Ibid., 209-10.

38. Ibid., 132.

39. Ibid., 136-37.

40. Ibid., 129.

41. Ibid., 129-30.

42. Ibid., 164.

43. Ibid.

44. Lash, *Eleanor and Franklin,* 414.

45. "Factory Plan in Hill Colony Stirs Protest," *Washington Post,* 5 Dec. 1933.

46. Cook, *Eleanor Roosevelt: Volume Two,* 144.

47. Ward, *A New Deal for America,* 74.

48. Ibid., 75.

49. Ibid.

50. Cook, *Eleanor Roosevelt: Volume Two,* 147.

51. Ward, *A New Deal for America,* 112.

52. Lash, *Eleanor and Franklin,* 408.

53. Ibid., 413.

54. Eleanor Roosevelt, *This I Remember,* 132-33.

55. Lash, *Eleanor and Franklin,* 411.

56. Ibid., 413.

57. Roosevelt, *This I Remember,* 132-33.

58. Lash, *Eleanor and Franklin,* 417.

BIBLIOGRAPHY

Articles and Books

Black, Allida, ed. *Courage in a Dangerous World: The Political Writings of Eleanor Roosevelt.* New York: Columbia University Press, 1999.

Bondi, Victor. *American Decades: 1930-1939.* Detroit: Gale Research, 1995.

Caroli, Betty Boyd. *The Roosevelt Women.* New York: Basic Books, 1998.

Clapp, Elsie Ripley. *Community Schools in Action.* New York: Viking Press, 1939.

Cook, Blanche Wiesen. *Eleanor Roosevelt: Volume One, 1884-1933.* New York: Viking Penguin, 1992.

Cook, Blanche Wiesen. *Eleanor Roosevelt: Volume Two, 1933-1938.* New York: Viking, 1999.

Davis, Kenneth S. *FDR: The New Deal Years, 1933-1937.* New York: Random House, 1986.

"Diary of a Homesteader's Wife." *Liberty* (2 January 1937): 12.

Faber, Doris. *Eleanor Roosevelt: First Lady of the World.* New York: Puffin Books, 1986.

"Factory Plan in Hill Colony Stirs Protest," *Washington Post,* 5 Dec. 1933.

Freedman, Russell. *Eleanor Roosevelt: A Life of Discovery.* New York: Clarion Books, 1993.

Haid, Stephen Edward. "Arthurdale: An Experiment in Community Planning, 1933-1947." Ph.D. diss. West Virginia University, 1975.

Kreiser, Christine M. "'I Wonder Whom God Will Hold Responsible': Mary Behner and the Presbyterian Mission on Scotts Run." *West Virginia History,* Volume 53, 1994.

Lash, Joseph P. *Dealers and Dreamers*. New York: Doubleday, 1988.

Lash, Joseph P. *Eleanor and Franklin: The Story of Their Relationship Based on Eleanor Roosevelt's Private Papers*. New York: W.W. Norton & Company, Inc., 1971.

Lee, Sidney D. *"And the Trees Cried."* Morgantown, W.Va.: Sidney D. Lee, 1991.

"Monthly Narrative Report, Sept. 25, 1937." RG 96, National Archives.

Nardo, Don. *The Great Depression*. San Diego: Greenhaven Press, 1998.

Pharr, T.R. Memorandum. Eleanor Roosevelt Papers, series 70, Franklin D. Roosevelt Library, Hyde Park, N.Y.

Roosevelt, Eleanor. *Eleanor Roosevelt's My Day: Her Acclaimed Columns, 1936-1945*. New York: Pharos Books, 1949.

Roosevelt, Eleanor. *This I Remember*. New York: Harper & Brothers, 1949.

Roosevelt, Eleanor. *You Learn By Living: Eleven Keys for a More Fulfilling Life*. New York: Harper, 1960.

Stewart, Gail B. *The New Deal*. New York: New Discovery Books, 1993.

Ward, Bryan, ed. *A New Deal for America: Proceedings from a National Conference on New Deal Communities*. Arthurdale, W.Va.: Arthurdale Heritage, Inc., 1995.

Audio and Video Tapes

"Arthurdale: A First Lady's Legacy" documentary produced by WNPB, Morgantown, West Virginia Public Broadcasting, 1988.

Oral histories of the homesteaders: interviews done by West Virginia University Regional History and Archives, Morgantown, West Virginia.

Personal Interviews

Bonnette, Jennifer. Conversation with author, Arthurdale, W.Va., 25 November 1999.

Day, Bob and Edna. Conversation with author, Arthurdale, W.Va., 25 November 1999.

Hornyak, Deanna. Conversation with author, Arthurdale, W.Va., 27 May 2000.

Mayor, Annabelle. Conversation with author, Arthurdale, W.Va., 25 November 1999.

Roscoe, Joe. Conversation with author, Arthurdale, W.Va., 25 November 1999.

Shine, Paulette. Conversation with author, Osage, W.Va., 27 May 2000.

Williams, Glenna. Conversation with author, Arthurdale, W.Va., 25 November 1999.

INDEX